CHAPTER 1
"FORGET BEING A RE

IT was the summer of 1959 and I was close to having my final lesson at Nantymoel Secondary School before stepping into the world of work.

I was among several other 15-year-olds who waited rather nervously outside the headmaster's room for an interview with a school leaving officer.

A scholar I was not.

I was a moron at maths, I could never get to grips with geography and hopeless when it came to history but I did take a shine to English lessons.

And then came my turn to face the officer.

"Now then boy," he said eyeing me up and down, "what are your working plans when you leave school?"

"I want to be a newspaper reporter sir."

A reply which brought a bit of a cough, a tilt of the head and more of a smirk than a smile from the officer.

"I'm sorry but you can forget that. You are never going to be a newspaper reporter because you will never get the qualifications needed.

"Now what about an engineering apprenticeship at one of the factories down on the trading estate or perhaps a job on the council?"

I was not interested.

I had ended up in a Secondary Modern school after failing the Grammar School which left my mam broken hearted.

She had been up the Co-op and ordered the Grammar School blazer and tie which I never got to wear.

She was inconsolable, all her hopes of me being a doctor or solicitor had gone out of the middle room window.

The lady next door did come into offer words of comfort. "Don't worry," she said to mam,"as long as he can get a job days regular and count his change he will be alright."
I can remember leaving that interview underwhelmed but not undaunted.
 I wasn't cut out to be an engineering apprentice I was going to be a newspaper reporter full stop.
Little did I know it then but it would It take me more than 30 jobs later to realise that dream.

A LETTER FROM BENNY HILL.

AS I drifted from job to job I never lost the desire to put pen to paper.
I think it was at the time I was working at the TC Jones factory in Treorchy in 1972 spraying red oxide on girders when I thought I could make some shekels writing gags for popular comedian Benny Hill.
So one night I sat on the couch and jotted down some sketches I thought Mr Hill could use in his popular TV show. Sketches like:"An oil tanker on a motorway runs out of petrol " and "A lorry load of tyres coming to a halt because of a puncture"
Terrible I know but I thought Benny could put them to some good use.
I posted off my sketches to the ATV studios hoping that they would catch Benny's eye.
A few weeks passed when I received a handwritten envelope which when I opened contained a handwritten note from Benny Hill which read:
"Dear David,
Thank you for the sketches but I won't be using them because I have my own gag writer.

PS:You should have included an SAE (stamped addressed envelope)".
Sorry Benny.Oh Well! Back to spraying girders it was.

MY JOB AS A "RUNNER."

IT was at a football match at Ynys Park, Ton Pentre when a chance conversation put me on the first step of the reporting ladder.

I was there with a pal of mine called Mal Eggett when he started chatting to a chap by the name of Arthur "Jack" Trembath.

I discovered later that Rhondda born Jack Trembath was a freelance reporter and also a rugby correspondent for the Sunday People.

He also provided coverage of Welsh league football to the Sunday Nationals and was also a great support to Treorchy born football referee Clive Thomas.

During their conversation Mal happened to mention that I nursed an ambition to be a newspaper reporter.

"Is that so," said Jack," how would you like to help out my reporting team?"

Of course I jumped at the writing chance.

And so on Saturday afternoons I met up with Arthur's brother Hedley Trembath who did the reports on Pontypridd RFC's home matches for the Sunday Nationals.

I was what was called a "runner" for Hedley.

He would write up the reports and I would telephone them over to the Sunday newspapers.

To say things would get a bit hectic was an understatement. With just one phone plugged into a point under the grandstand every Sunday newspaper not only wanted "running copy" during the match but also reports on the final whistle.

In those days Ponty played their home matches at Ynysyngharad Park and included in the team then were Bob Penberthy, Tom David, Joe Smith, Colin Bolderson, Jeff Hazzard, Brian Juliff and Dai Legge.

For the next couple of years I phoned reports to the News of the World, the People and Sunday Mirror among others all the while itching to whip out my biro and start scribbling.

My hopes were given a boost when I was given a break as a runner at the Ponty rugby matches after Jack asked me to do reports on Welsh League football matches for the old "Pink" Football Echo.

MY REPORTS IN "THE PINK".

THE Football "Pink" Echo had been produced since 1919 and published match results from Saturday afternoon games in South Wales.

It meant that on Saturday afternoons I would travel to Ton Pentre, Ferndale, Tonyrefail and Blaenrhondda football clubs to phone over a 50 words half time report and full time score to the Echo sportdesk.

I met some remarkable people including Ferndale secretary Glyn Lewis and Ton Pentre's Tommy "Alf" Davies.

Always had a warm welcome from Glyn who to me epitomised the meaning of a clubman.

Close friend and loyal assistant Roy Cooper said: "He was a mild-mannered man and a wonderful friend.

"If you cut Glyn in half, you would find Ferndale AFC at the centre.

"I don't think he ever got the recognition he deserved in the game."

I can well remember loitering near a newsagents on a Saturday evening waiting for the Football Echo to be delivered so I could read my report.

MY OTHER NAME WAS TED EDWARDS.

IN 1974 Pontypridd RFC were re-located to a new venue at Sardis Road.

The move had come about following the re-development of the A470 trunk road near the Ynysyngharad ground.

It also proved a good move for me because I finally I got my chance of writing a full match report and I loved it full stop.

It was while covering the Ponty matches that I came into contact with Jim Campbell, the editor of the Pontypridd and Llantrisant Observer and also the Rhondda Leader.

We had sat next to each other in the press box for a couple of weeks when he asked me if I would like to "do a bit of sports writing" for the local newspapers.

"I'd love to," I said.

The sports desk at the Welsh Harp building in Pontypridd was occupied by Bob Phillips, who would eventually net a successful career as a soccer correspondent with the BBC.

I did a football column for Bob called "On the Ball" which was a round up of all the gossip surrounding the Welsh League clubs in the area.

I also carved my name with typing pride on a rugby column called "Scrum Down with Ted Edwards".

Because I wasn't part of the reporting staff I could not use my proper name so the editor decided to change David to Ted and to this day some rugby players of a past era call me Ted.

PHIL AND SARDIS SCENE.

IT was the same for my writing pal Phil Caddy who reported under the name Phil David.

For many years Phil regularly supplied coverage for the sports pages of the Leader.

In the days when the Leader was a broadsheet, Phil, who died in 2011, used to supply reports on rugby,football and cricket.

Phil also penned a popular rugby column called Sardis Scene which gave the lowdown on all that was happening at the Ponty rugby club.

Every Sunday I would ring around the soccer and rugby clubs for the weekly columns and one of my regular contacts then was Ian Pritchard who was the coach of Cilfynydd RFC.

Ian and I became close pals and I was devastated at his sudden death.

When I wasn't putting pen to paper at rugby matches I was putting pen to paper booking in deliveries at my job as a back door security officer at the Pontypridd based Ynysybwl Co-op.

One Monday morning when delivering my columns to the newspaper office at the Welsh Harp Jim Campbell invited me into his office for a chat.

He told me that Bob Phillips was leaving for pastures new and he would like me to be the next person to sit at his desk.

"You mean as a full time reporter?" I asked.

"Sure do," answered Jim.

But there were problems.

PART OF THE UNION.

I was 38 years old and the NUJ (National Union of Journalists) may have something to say about the matter and I would also have to attend a course at Cardiff College of Further Education to achieve a post graduate degree in Journalism.

To attend the course I would have to quit my security job at the Co-op and that worried me because I had a family to support and if I failed the course I could end up jobless.

After getting the green light from the Union I took a reporting gamble and signed up for the course.

I knew there maybe trouble ahead the first morning I sat among 18 and 19-year-olds to be introduced to the lecturer. He wanted to know everyone's education background and I started to squirm in my seat when the first young wannabe reporter named the university he attended.

"Didn't Prince Charles attend that one?" asked the lecturer.

A few universities later it came to my turn.

"And where did you attend?"

"Nantymoel Secondary Modern sir."

"I'm sorry I didn't catch that,"

"Nantymoel Secondary Modern."

I don't know whether he believed me or not.

For three long months my 38-year-old brain struggled to keep pace with the under 20-year-olds who were also sitting the course.

I had to burn the midnight paraffin oil to study shorthand, law, newspaper practice, court reporting and feature writing among others.

I will never forget the morning I was overwhelmed with relief to be told that I had just scraped in getting my diploma.

And so I swapped my Co-op security keys for typewriter keys to start my long awaited journey into journalism.

A REPORTER AT LAST.

THE Welsh Harp in Pontypridd was a rather imposing building which housed the South Wales Echo reporters on the ground floor and Celtic Newspapers (Rhondda Leader, Pontypridd Observer and Llantrisant Observer) on the second floor.

Among the reporters then were Judith Davies, Pearl Penrose, Jean Parry, Haydn Price, Phil Howells and Judith Marsh.

IN 1983 Bob Phillips, packed in his sports desk job with the Leader and I got to sit in his office seat at the Welsh Harp office.

Bob taught me a lot about sports reporting and I will always be grateful for that.

And so it was the start of some memorable sports reporting moments.

One of my first tasks was reporting on a home football match involving Ton Pentre FC.

I had a great welcome at Ton and enjoyed reporting on the game.

Not so on my second visit to Ynys Park.

I had only put one step inside the park gate when I was ordered to appear before the committee who were sat waiting for me in the clubhouse.

There I was stood in front of some committee members who had the Rhondda Leader newspaper containing my report on the match in front of them.

And then there were the questions.

"Explain what you meant by saying this player should have done better? and "What do you mean saying this defender was at fault?" and so it went on.

I couldn't believe it-I felt like I was in front of a Junta.

My defence was:"I wrote it as I saw it."

But to be football fair after that cross examination was over it never happened again and I was always made welcome at Ynys Park.

During those soccer days there was one Welsh League footballer I'll never forget.

For me Gerald Sweeney was the most colourful character in the Welsh League all those kick offs ago.

My one outstanding memory of Gerald was when I was covering a match between Ferndale and visiting Ton Pentre which was always a dynamic derby.

Gerald had played for Ton Pentre and when he scored against his old club he took his shirt off and ran up the bank at the Ferndale ground onto the main road and waved it above his head in sheer delight.

What a character.

"FIGHTING TALK."

THEN there was the night I was covering an amateur boxing event.

It was an enjoyable evening until one of the last fights of the night when all boxing hell was let loose.

The ref had stepped in to part the two young boxers to give them some words of advice when without warning one of the youngsters sneakily punched the other one.

That was the signal for fighting to erupt all over the packed venue.

While it was all going on the trainer of the host boxing club said:"Dave please don't report this because it will look bad on the club."

"Sorry but I have to," I replied, "but it will only be published in the Llantrisant Observer."

As was my reporting duty the clubhouse brawl was a lead story in the next issue of the Llantrisant Observer.

The following Sunday morning I received an early morning call from that very same boxing trainer.

"Have you seen the News of the World?" he angrily asked.

"No I haven't. Is there a problem?"

"A big problem," he ranted, "the boxing brawl is splashed over a news page. Why did you have to do that?"

"But I didn't do it."

The report had been done by a freelance reporter who made a living by buying up all the weekly newspapers and selecting the juiciest stories and flogging them on to the Nationals.

I did eventually convince the trainer that it was not me and we remained the best of boxing pals.

And then there was the time......

But that's another story.

DUDLEY WAS THE HEADLINER.

I saw off a few editors during my years with the Rhondda Leader however there was one who stood a banner headline above the rest.

His name was Dudley Stephens.

Dudley became the editor of the combined Rhondda Leader, Pontypridd Observer and Llantrisant Observer back in 1985.

Born in Ynysddu Dudley had ended up in the editor's chair in the Welsh Harp after enjoying a successful career in Fleet Street, including working for the Daily Sketch as a Parliamentary correspondent before it merged with the Daily Mail.

He was also a reporter with the South Wales Argus and South Wales Echo.

An avid reader Dudley, who sadly died in 2012, was also a brilliant chess player becoming a Welsh junior champion at the age of 18.

I loved being in Dudley's company. He was a brilliant talker and also a brilliant listener.

I always said that if I was on the TV show "Who wants to be a Millionaire?" and needed to phone a friend then it would have definitely been Dud.

Even after we both retired we would regularly meet up in Alfreds Bar and Grill in Pontypridd and put the newspaper world to rights.

Dud always had some great stories to tell.

Here's one of them.

When he was working in Fleet Street he, along with two reporter pals, decided to go for a night out on the town.

And they didn't half give the booze a battering.

Eventually the tanked up trio made it to a flat belonging to one of them.

Once inside they collapsed in a drunken stupor on a settee and chairs.

A couple of hours later Dudley was suddenly woken up by one of his still drunken pals who pointed at a TV set which had been left on.

"Hey Dud," he slurred pointing at the TV screen," look at her she's gorgeous.How beautiful is she?"
I'd love to take her out."
With bleary half asleep eyes Dudley managed to set his sight on the screen.
"You idiot," he said," that's Lady Penelope.She's a puppet."
Thunderbirds was being shown on the telly.
And then there was the time that Dudley was sub editing a news story.
"Hey Dave," he shouted across the office," I've got a story here about a woman from Glyncoch who has teamed up with a chap from Ynysybwl to start a business venture.
"Now that is what I call a 'Coch and 'Bwl story."
Brilliant.
I miss Dud.

THE KEY TO A CODE.

IN those early reporting days after I had finished a typewritten story it was handed to the editor who would check it over for any mistakes along with a word count. The story, called hard copy, was placed in an envelope along with others ready to be collected by a van which was then taken to the Celtic printworks in Dowlais where it was checked again by sub editors.
There was a steady stream of trainee reporters at the Welsh Harp in the early 1980s.
One in particular I remember who on one occasion not only had Dudley mystified but also the sub editors in Dowlais.
The van for collecting the envelopes had arrived and the trainee was struggling to finish his story.
When he had put In hIs last full stop the editor stuffed it into an envelope and handed it to the van driver.

Later that day the editor received a phone call from the chief sub editor.

"I have got a story in front of me which has been written in code," he said.

"In code?" asked Dudley.

"Yes, it's gibberish. We can't figure it out."

A very puzzled editor asked the trainee how he had written the story.

To which he replied:"The E on my typewriter wasn't working so I used the next letter along which was the R."

Dudley was laughing too much to give him a ticking off.

HATCHES, MATCHES AND DESPATCHES.

THERE was one band of people who had my utmost respect during my years with the Leader.

The District Correspondents.

I always believed the District News was the pulse of the paper.

Readers wanted to know what was happening in their neck of the woods.

It was all about hatches, matches and despatches. (births, marriages and deaths).

But sometimes things can go wrong in the District News pages which I found out back in the early 1980s.

The Rhondda Leader office was based in the Welsh Harp, Pontypridd back in those days and the paper used to come out on a Wednesday morning.

One particular Wednesday morning I was the first to arrive at the office where I saw a little old lady and two burly blokes, who I later found out were her two sons, standing by the front door.

"Can I help?" I asked.

"I've just read about my death in the District News," she said, waving the newspaper in front of me, while the sons gave me looks that I felt that people could soon be reading about my death in the newspaper.

Just then the editor arrived and as soon as he realised what had happened he raided the petty cash and sent me scarpering over to Ponty town centre to get the biggest box of chocolates I could find and also a ginormous bouquet of flowers to try and make sure the old lady was glad to be alive.

But I suppose it can happen.

You know what the valley grapevine is like?

So and so is firstly "very ill" then "not much hope left" then "sinking fast" and by the time it reached the correspondent "DEAD" even though the person is still alive and just about kicking.

Just part of a reporting life with the Rhondda Leader.

In 1986 the reporting staff packed away their pencils and notebooks and headed across the Ponty highway to a new office location in Taff Street, Pontypridd.

And then came along another big change in my fledging life as a reporter.

It was called new technology.

Gone was my typewriter to be replaced by a computer and no longer were my stories going to be stored as "hard copy". They were going to be stored on a floppy disc.

CHAPTER 2
THE WRITING ON THE WALL.

I WILL never forget the first news story I did back in 1984. A chap had contacted the Welsh Harp office complaining that the council had painted a garden wall either side of his house but not his and he was not happy about it.

I was despatched by the editor to call on this bloke, who lived on his own, to find out why the Council had given his garden wall the brush off.

I arrived at his house and after knocking on the door he shouted:"Come in".

There he was sat in a chair with his arm in a sling his foot in a plaster cast and a surgical collar around his neck.

Of course being an ace reporter my first question was:"Don't mind me asking but have you had some sort of accident?"

He told me that he had been to a funeral a few days earlier and whilst walking in the cemetery he slipped and fell.

An ambulance eventually arrived and while transporting him to the hospital a car pulled out of a side street forcing the ambulance to brake suddenly which ended up with him having a whiplash injury.

By some miracle nothing more happened to him before he got to the hospital where it was discovered that he not only had a whiplash injury but also a broken bone in his foot and a fractured collarbone.

I couldn't believe it.

Here I was doing a story about an unpainted garden wall while in front of me was the unluckiest man unable to walk the Rhondda streets.

Despite my efforts, and not by accident, it was the unpainted garden wall that ended up on a Leader page.

THE NINE STONE COWBOY.

AND of course the planned Cowboy Theme park in the valley provided the Leader with a stetson full of stories.
Billed as Westernworld on the site of the old Fernhill colliery it was all set for the good, the bad and the ugly cowboys to ride into the black hills of Blaenrhondda.
Supposedly inspired by Dolly Parton's Dollywood resort in Tennessee the £1million development was opened in May 1987.
But before the first gunfight got underway bit the dust a few weeks later.
There was a parade which included a wagon train and cowboys and indians which blazed a valley trail from the council offices in Pentre to the green hills of Blaenrhondda.
The parade was led by a fully badged sheriff to launch the venture and when the reporter got back to the office after covering the event the editor asked him to describe the sheriff.
"Was he big or small fat or thin?" he asked.
"About average I suppose. He wasn't all that big," he replied.
So the story about the sheriff ran under the headline:"The Nine Stone Cowboy" which I thought was brilliant.
I can recall doing a telephone interview with one of the Birmingham based entrepreneurs involved in the venture.
He told me that he was excited about the theme park's future and there were no cash problems because all the funding was in place.
Methinks he spoke with forked tongue.
Westernworld was the start of more planned theme parks for the valley which sadly never got off the ground.

COLLIN'S CANINE MESSAGE

THERE was the story I did about a young rugby player named Collin Smith who lived in Tonyrefail at the time.

Collin was an outstanding young rugby player but at the age of 15 his boyhood dreams of perhaps one day playing for Wales were shattered following an injury during a youth game.

Collin had fractured his leg but although he knew it was an injury that would sideline him for months he would be able to return to playing rugby again.

But that would never happen.

The injury quickly changed from a fracture to a life threatening situation when it was discovered that dog's mess on the rugby field had infected Collin's injury and within 24 hours part of his leg had to be amputated which meant a five months stay in hospital.

I recently met Collin, who works for a brewery company, and he was looking well.

We talked about that horrific event which happened more than 30 years ago and how he dealt with it.

The loss of part of his leg did not result in Collin's loss of love of rugby nor of dogs.

Dog's mess left by careless owners is never out of the news these days and the message from myself and Collin is:"Please pick your dog's mess up."

A CHAT WITH FREEDOM FIGHTER TOMMY.

There was also the time I interviewed former freedom fighter Tommy Adlam who had a remarkable story to tell.

Almost 50 years ago young Rhondda men boarded valley trains and under a cloak of secrecy arrived in Spain 48 hours later.

They were members of the International Brigade, a handful of freedom fighters committed to helping the Spanish peasants battle against the mighty armies of General Franco.

This is Tom Adlam's story told to me in 1986.

"The Spaniard ripped his white neck tie off and began waving it frantically.

Tom Adlam sprang toward the agitated figure and grabbed him by the throat.

"No Surrender. Comprende?" he snarled, "you try that again and I'll knock your block off".

The trembling Spaniard jabbed his finger behind Adlam's shoulder and the terrified look in his eyes made the Welshman spin around.

Adlam froze as he stared down at the muzzle of a machine gun which an Italian soldier was coiled over.

The gun had jammed.

For several seconds the Rhondda miner stared death in the face as the Italian tried to free the gun's mechanism.

After two long and bitter years of battling against the tyrannous regime of General Franco the Civil War had finally ended for the St John Ambulance man from Upper Alma Place in Pentre.

Ahead lay a prisoner of war compound or even death.

Even as a schoolboy Adlam always had an air of defiance and this remained with him when as a 14-year-old he went to work underground at the Abergorki colliery.

In 1932 Adlam found himself out of work when the colliery closed and for several years he languished on the dole queues.

Meanwhile in July 1936 unrest in Spain had erupted into a Civil War when the peasants formed a ragged undisciplined army and rebelled against the mighty armies of Franco.
At that time Adlam was a member of the Communist Party and was active in his local group making collections and trying to support the oppressed people in every way possible
However for Adlam and some of his friends fundraising simply wasn't enough they needed to do more.
On a Saturday morning in 1937 Adlam and some of his pals met at Ystrad railway station and bought tickets for Cardiff. They finally reached Paris and then went on to the south of France.
The following night they were smuggled by schooner into Barcelona before travelling to Valencia where other freedom fighters were collected before being taken to Albacete.
The 26-year-old from Pentre was eager to get to the battle front but when the group leaders realised he had first aid qualifications he was immediately detailed to help the injured and the dying.
While carrying out his duties his only means of defence was an outdated Russian rifle which was typical of the weaponry of the People's Army.
Although mentally and physically drained the Rhondda freedom fighter stayed at the battle front until his body could take no more and he was taken to a makeshift hospital.
After two weeks respite Adlam was detailed to take charge of the raw Spanish recruits who were being sent to the battle front.
One night when Adlam and his band of recruits were camped near a farm he sensed something was wrong.

Just before dawn a Spanish officer ordered Adlam to retrieve an ambulance and as he set off he looked back to see the worried look on the faces of the recruits.

He hadn't got very far when an enemy tank swung into view and all hell broke loose.

He sprinted back towards the group screaming at them to take cover.

With the jammed machine gun pointing towards them they managed to reach the shelter of some nearby trees.

It was then that an Italian officer approached staring coldy at them.

"Internationale?" he shouted jabbing his finger towards Adlam.

"English, " said Adlam defiantly.

"Inglese," sneered the officer undoing his gun holster strap.

Adlam believed death was just seconds away as the Italian raised his gun and pointed it towards his head.

Defiantly Adlam lifted his bowed head and stared the officer in the face.

"Go on-shoot."

He heard the blast of the gun before collapsing in a heap. Was death this painless?

The officer had deliberately fired the gun over Adlam's head. After what seemed an eternity the officer barked at Adlam to get to his feet before putting his gun back in his holster and walking away.

Adlam and the other prisoners were then ordered to march to a nearby barracks where they were held prisoner until the war ended and he was repatriated.

WHAT A WELCOME FOR JOCKY.

I will never forget the time I was banned from Tynewydd Labour Club.

And it was all because of the events which unfolded one October night back in the 1980s.

The club was the venue for the final of the Rhondda Leader Darts championship and the special guest at the event was World Darts champion Jocky Wilson.

The Rhondda Leader Darts Championship was a popular event way back then with players from all over the valley taking part.

Also attending the event were Celtic newspaper big wigs including the managing director, editor in chief and circulation manager among others who were gathered in an upstairs room

"You Welsh people are wonderful," Jocky told a packed audience,"it's a pleasure to be here."

Jocky was more than happy to give an interview after an exhibition match although he asked the photographer to delay taking pictures because of the camera flash.

Barely 20 minutes after giving his speech the wee Scot was swiftly ushered out of the main hall which had erupted into one "hell of a ding dong."

It looked like something out of a cowboy film with fists flying, chairs and tables upturned and shattered glasses everywhere.

I managed to get past the blood, sweat and booze to race upstairs and get hold of my editor.

We got downstairs and the when the editor poked his head around the corner a beer bottle flew past him.

"What do you want me to do?" I asked him.

"Report it all," he said," and make sure you get plenty of pictures".

Despite appeals from a club committee man to stop the fracas what should have been a special evening was destroyed and soon ended.

The story under the front page banner headline "Rhondda's Night of Shame" along with pictures of the punch ups appeared in the next issue of the Leader and the circulation figures for that week were sky high.

The club committee were not happy about the story and pictures and the editor was told that I was banned from the club along with the photographer who they claimed had "choreographed the fight" by standing on a chair encouraging people to throw more punches.

I ask you?

The events of that night put an end to the Rhondda Leader Darts championship.

And that's no bull.

KEVIN'S HEART WARMING STORY.

Here's one story I never get tired of telling because I suppose it was so meaningful.

It was what you call in the newspaper game "a heart warming" story.

Back in 1985 I wrote a story about Kevin Moon who was the Leader at Ton and Gelli Boys Club.

Kevin needed publicity for a sponsored basketball match he was planning aimed at raising much needed funds for the club.

Some weeks after the story was published Kevin was surprised and shocked to receive a parcel from a prisoner In an English jail.

The valley born prisoner had the Rhondda Leader delivered to him every week and read the story about Kev's fundraising match.

Inside the parcel was a money box and cruet set he had made from used matchsticks

There was also a letter to Kev on HM Prison headed paper. It read:" I have the Rhondda Leader delivered to my prison cell every week and I read about your appeal for funds for your club.

"I can't send you cash but I hope the money box and cruet set will help in some way.

"Perhaps you could raffle them or put them up for auction." Although many miles away under very different circumstances the prisoner said his heart was very much in the Rhondda and he wanted to do his best to help valley youngsters.

He ended his letter by giving Kev and the Boys Clubs' committee his best wishes and signed it "Rhondda Boy."

I remember Kevin was really knocked out by the gesture. He said: "This guy must have taken a lot of time and a lot of care to make these and he has done them for the Boys Club."

BRUCE WAS A PIED PIPER.

I will never forget the years that the Rhondda became "Little America".

I think it was 1983 when I got a call to say that there was a "big black basketball bloke" walking around Treorchy.

And that led to my first meeting with 6'7" Bruce Crump, who must have been around 17 stone soaking wet and who had flown in from Florida to play basketball for what would become the Just Rentals team.

Bruce had never jogged far from his Jacksonville home before arriving in the valley.

I called Bruce the Pied Piper of the Rhondda because wherever he went kids would follow.

And they were always full of questions like:"What do they call pavements in America Bruce?"

"Sidewalks," he would drawl

"And what do they call sweets?"

"Candy".

And on it went.

After returning to his Jacksonville home after his playing stint in the Rhondda it was decided to bring Bruce back for another term.

The news that Bruce was coming back was picked up by BBC Radio Wales and I was contacted by them and asked for a telephone number for Bruce because they wanted to interview him at his home in America.

Before I agreed I checked with my editor whether to give the telephone number.

He said:"Before you give out the number contact Bruce and tell him that during the interview he must mention the Rhondda Leader".

And so I got in touch with Bruce and told him about the planned interview and to mention the Rhondda Leader.

The interview was aired on an early morning programme and typically of Bruce he mentioned the Rhondda Leader more than once.

The best line was when he said:"My mom is sat here reading the Rhondda Leader."

I wonder if it was the Letters page?

What a character.

The second American to set basketball trainers in the Rhondda was Dave Lawrence from North Carolina.
Dave proved to be a sensation with his dynamic slam dunk displays in the Rhondda Sports Centre which led to his nickname "Dai Dunker".
Dave became hugely popular during his time here and has always had a love affair with the Rhondda which he calls his "second home".
And then along came another awesome American, from South Carolina, called Andy "Beef" Williams who you just could not help but like.
Andy and Dave lived in a Ton Pentre flat and I remember dropping by because I needed to speak to Dave.
Dave was not in so I asked Andy if he knew where he was.
"He's gone to see someone in Texas street," said he.
Texas Street? I soon realised that he meant Matexa Street in Ton Pentre.
And I will never forget La Verne Evans who went to play in Portugal after his playing stint in the Rhondda ended.
When La Verne was driven from a London airport to the Rhondda while travelling through Penygraig he said to the driver:"I guess this is what you call downtown."
Downtown?
After more than 30 years I have been in contact with them again and they all say they have brilliant memories of the long gone years they spent in the Rhondda and always want to be remembered to fans and friends.

GO GET HIM CHRIS.

TO mark the arrival of Dave Lawrence a special match between the Just Rentals team and a Rhondda Leader select team was held at the Ystrad Sports Centre.

Included in the Rhondda Leader team (which I was the coach to) was Tommy David, Chris Seldon, Alan Rose and Bob Penberthy.

It was the first time the Rhondda fans would see Dave Lawrence in action and boy oh boy were they in for a shock. In the first few minutes he just leapt sky high and performed a super slam dunk which was the first of many.

The fans went from jaw dropping to jubilation as Lawrence delighted them with his skills on court.

Meanwhile on the bench Tommy David was trying to figure out how to stop Lawrence.

Would it be a zone defence or maybe try a zone offence? Chris Seldon came up with the solution straightaway.

"Let me on there Tom," he said,"I'll sort him out."

It was then that Tom had to remind Chris that this was a "friendly."

Tom probably had to explain to Chris what a "friendly" was.

A THUNDER OF DAPS.

There was always a thunder of daps whenever the annual Rhondda Fun Run saw thousands take to the valley streets. It was one of the highlights of the reporting year for me.

Myself and a photographer would be all set at the Rhondda Sports Centre for the race start and then jump in a car to snap up the runners at different locations.

The day before the Fun Run co-founder Selwyn Jones with megaphone in hand would tour the valley asking people to be ready with bottles of water to keep the runners cool.

Anyway myself and the photographer were primed for taking pictures at a valley spot which saw the runners take on an incline.

This poor dab was obviously struggling up the incline when an elderly lady stepped out of the doorway and threw a bucket of water over him.

Shocked and soaking wet he somehow managed to stagger up the hill.

I never did find out if he finished the race.

GOLDEN MEMORIES.

I'VE lost count of the number of Golden Weddings I covered during my reporting years with the Leader.

Whenever we were made aware that a couple were about to celebrate 50 years of marriage it was mostly down to me and a photographer to pay a visit.

After the photographer had got the couple to cwtch close together on a couch for a picture it was time for me to put pen to pad.

And of course the 64,000 dollar question was always:"What is the secret of a long and happy marriage?"

And I had heard all the answers including:"Never go to bed on a quarrel."

"It's give and take.I give and she takes."

"We have always been the best of friends."

But there was one Golden Wedding that sticks in my memory.

I asked the big question to which the lady replied:"We have never had a quarrel."

"Really," said me,"not in 50 years of marriage."

"Not a cross word,"said she.

"And where was it you got married again?"

"Ponty Registry office. It was a terrible morning.Bucketed down with rain,"said she.

"No it didn't. It was a lovely morning there wasn't a drop of rain about," said he.
To which she replied:"What are you talking about?. It poured down all morning.."
They were still arguing when we left.

DENNIS AND THAT PICTURE.

BACK in the 1980s the editor came up with the bright idea to have a celebrity reading the Rhondda Leader.
And so a photographer and I were despatched to a pub in Bridgend where celebrities were meeting up before playing in a charity football match.
Among the celebrities was Dennis Waterman, one of the stars of the hit TV series "The Sweeney" and the editor told me that it had been arranged with the pub management that the Minder star would have his picture taken while reading the Rhondda Leader.
When we arrived in the pub car park I went in to check with the pub manager about setting up the picture.
To which he said:"I don't know what you are talking about. I haven't made any arrangement about a Dennis Waterman picture."
That was something that caused me and the photographer a rather big problem.
Somehow or other I had to get the picture taken.
Shortly afterwards a car swept into the car park and out got Dennis Waterman. We had only taken a few steps towards him when he turned and said: "No photographs now go away" or Sweeney words to that effect.
Not long afterwards another car arrived and out stepped Rhondda born World Cup football referee Clive Thomas who fortunately knew me.

When I told Clive about the problem over the picture he said: "Give me a couple of minutes."
In no time Clive stepped out of the pub with not a happy looking Mr Waterman who gave me a Minder glare and said: "What do you want?"
He did agree to have his picture taken reading the newspaper and afterwards said:"What is this stuff all about?"
When I looked I could see he was reading the District News pages.
After the picture was done he was great and spent time giving me an interview along with a few laughs.

CHAPTER 3

VALLEY'S TITANIC CONNECTION.

BELIEVE it or not sometimes you can pick up a good story from a cemetery.

In 1984 I was told that in Treorchy cemetery there was a grave dedicated to a Rhondda miner called Dai Bowen who had perished in the Titanic.

It was a story I very much wanted to write.

And so I penned a two part feature about Rhondda miners Les Williams and Dai Bowen who perished when the Titanic sank in 1912.

With the Internet very much not available in those days my research involved trips to the library and trying to find out what the Rhondda was like more than 100 years ago.

Les Williams, a 24-year-old blacksmith from Tonypandy, pushed open the door of the New Inn hotel in Ton Pentre and peered in at a sea of gaunt faced, frail,cloth capped figures huddled together around the stove.

Some racked up dust flecked phlegm and spat it onto the coals, a sizzling legacy of their mining trade.

"Who are you fighting tonight Les?"asked Dai Bowen, a 21-year-old collier who lived in Baglan Street,Treherbert.

"Kid Hughes, from Clydach,"grunted the powerfully built Williams,"I don't want to hang about too long,there's a lot to do."

"Aye~ agreed his pal,"I'm due at a Trealaw Hotel for a fight.See you tomorrow butty."

The year was 1912 when the Rhondda teemed with collieries and men were made to exist on the pittance paid by the coal owners.

There was little hope for Rhondda folk then, a life with little pleasure where the main pre-occupation was to try and live "a bit decent."

The cluster of shops in Treorchy and Tonypandy and other busy valley townships plied their trade with great urgency. On display in Willie Llewellyn's shop in Tonypandy was a lump of coal with a first prize of £2 to anyone fortunate enough to guess its correct weight.

Meanwhile, at the Pavilion picture palace "Little Hackerschmidt", a champion wrestler was in action while a little light entertainment was supplied by Carl Howard billed as "a comic card."

There was another form of entertainment however which stimulated the minds of the hardened valley miners-the notorious mountain fights which took place on the Rhondda hills on Sunday mornings.

While devout worshippers flocked to their chapels and churches the rugged mountain fighters fought bloody bare fist contests.

Mountain men with names like "James Figg", "Hen Pearce The Game Chicken", "Bendigo" and "Big Ben Brain" were denounced from the chapel pulpits as "hellions and scoundrels."

There was no quarter asked and none given as these battled scarred men left the Rhondda hills stained with the blood and sweat of their epic fights.

It was here on the windswept Rhondda mountains that Les Williams and Dai Bowen got their first taste of the "fighting game."

The taste was bitter but the money sweet and they hungered for it from then on.

The two great pals managed to see a memorable fight at the Treorchy fair when Frank Craig the "Coffee Cooler" the world middleweight champion fought local hero Dai Rush. According to legend "The Rush", a murderous body puncher, caught the American with two punches to the midriff.

The first punch staggered him while the second sent him crashing through the canvas wall of the marquee for the prize of a few pence.

This then was Rhondda at the turn of the century when desperate but proud men would beat the living daylights out of each other for a few pence.

Les Williams and Dai Bowen were just two of the hungry fighters of this era and both knew that their future was in their fists.

The two butties would travel up and down the valley fighting in the booths and the pubs and even though still young men their bodies had sampled the rigors of the ruthless fight game.

And so it was in 1912 that providence smiled upon the two young Rhondda miners offering them the opportunity that they daren't even dream of.

The booming cities of America were being swept by the boxing epidemic and even the backwoods were giving birth to their own special breed of hungry fighters.

Young Americans put brawn before brain to escape the poverty and the thirst for great fights could not be whetted. But even in cities like New York, Chicago and Detroit the ambitious and astute boxing promoters became aware that in the valleys of South Wales lay a generation of young men who would fight their hearts out given the opportunity.

Cigar smoking, beer swilling, boxing promoters had heard stories of men like Jimmy Wilde and Jim Driscoll who had become Welsh legends.

So arrangements were made to find out just what was happening in "them thar hills of Wales".

In January of 1912 an agent for an American promoter sat in the corner of a Rhondda hotel.

"You guys wanna a drink?" he asked.

Hollow faces turned and gazed in astonishment at the well dressed stranger, who looked rather out of place in the gloomy surroundings of the valley pub.

"Say Is there a fight taking place here tonight?" he asked, "I'd sure like to grab some of the action."

During the next few days the man from across the sea saw several fighters in action including Les Williams and Dai Bowen.

He asked the two miners to meet him in a valley public house.

"I got a proposition for you guys," he said, "How'd you like to fight in America?"

Dai Bowen's 20-year-old heart pounded at the American boxing promoter's offer.

" You really mean that?" he asked excitedly, " You want me to go and fight in America."

"Sure I do," he said, then after a pause, "What about your pal?"

Les Williams, a 24-year-old blacksmith from Tonypandy, sat silently idly swirling the last dregs of beer in his glass

"I don't know what to say about it" he murmured.

"Come on Les this is something we have always dreamed of."

"It's alright for you Dai you're a single man but I've got a wife and young child to watch out for".
"But America is where the money is Les. The only future for us here are the pits and probably an early grave".
"I suppose I could go over there and make some money to give us a better future," said Les.
"Now you guys are talking," said the American, "I'll start making arrangements immediately."
It was an elated Dai Bowen who walked to his Treherbert home on that rainy April night with thoughts turning to a new boxing life in America.
Meanwhile Les Williams had other thoughts as he trudged towards his home in Primrose Street.
He didn't want to leave his wife and young son but he knew that if this had to be the sacrifice to give them a better life then he must take it.
" I don't want to end up in the Scotch colliery all my life," he thought as he pushed open his front door.
The American boxing promoter had fixed up the two miners with a passage to New York and half a dozen fights across the Atlantic.
"You can prepare to sail on a liner bound for America on April 8th," he told them.
"Hang on a minute, "said Bowen, "why can't we go on this brand new White Star liner which sails two days later?"
"What's the difference?" asked Williams, "all these ships are the same."
"No listen, " said Bowen, "This ship is in all the newspapers and magazines.

"It's going on her maiden voyage to New York and not only that she's got a huge gymnasium on board where we can train while travelling across the Atlantic".

"Oh well... I suppose we could cancel the other passage," said Williams.

"What is the name of this ship?" asked the American

"It's called the Titanic."

On the morning of April 10th 1912 the two miners laid their baggage on the Southampton dock and stared disbelievingly at the ship in front of them.

"She's unsinkable you know," said Bowen, as they boarded the White Star liner.

As the floating town left Southampton Bowen and Williams waved to the onlookers.

"I'm missing the Rhondda already," said Williams," I wonder how long it will be before we return home?"

The two men sat quietly in their third class compartment reflecting on the past and dreaming of the future while also getting used to the new experience of sailing on a liner.

On April 11th they both went in search of the ships gymnasium eager to prepare for the fights which lay ahead in America.

For the next two days they explored the liner which never ceased to astonish them.

Bowen and Williams were bathed in perspiration as they ended another rigorous training session in the ship's gym.

"That's enough I reckon for today," said Williams. "what say you we go for a stroll before turning in?"

The night was calm, clear and bitterly cold as the huge liner headed toward Newfoundland.

It was almost 11.40pm on April 14th, 1912, when Williams and Bowen were abruptly wakened from their sleep by a mighty rumbling sound.
"What in God's name is happening?" asked Bowen.
"We must have hit something," said Williams.
A huge iceberg had vent its wrath on the liner by tearing a huge gash along her side.
Already her days were numbered.
Down in third class Bowen and Williams were among a swarm of people milling around at the foot of the main staircase.
The two men were used to grave danger, they risked their lives every day in the pit.
"Looks bad Les," said Bowen, "I reckon it's every man for himself".
Gripping the hand of his pal from the Rhondda he said:"If I don't see you in New York I'll see you in Treorchy."
At 2.20 am on April 15th the Titanic sank.
The ship they said would never sink went quietly to her watery grave taking with her over 1,500 lives including those of two Rhondda miners.
They never recovered the body of David John Bowen but Les Williams is buried in a cemetery in Halifax, Nova Scotia.
Sadly Les Williams son, also called Les, was killed in the 1965 Cambrian pit explosion.

THE INCREDIBLE MIKE WARD.

ANOTHER feature I wrote that was very special to me was about the life and death of a close pal named Mike Ward.
It is a remarkable story in many ways.

Our friendship began back in 1975 when 20-year-old Mike swaggered into a warehouse in Talbot Green where I was working at the time.

He bristled with confidence and it didn't take me long to realise the new fair haired arrival needed to be one of life's winners.

Mike often rebelled against authority, he was very much his own man but he also had a terrific sense of humour.

We struck up a remarkable friendship.

He was the devil may care young man while I was the mature 30-year-old shop steward.

So strong was our friendship that Mike was the best man at my wedding.

When we had clocked our time cards at the warehouse for the final time we lost touch until one Summer's afternoon I happened to be strolling around an outdoor market in Llantrisant.

Suddenly from behind a stall bedecked with flowers emerged a beaming, tanned, Mike Ward.

Later I discovered that Mike gave away more flowers than he sold.

We promised to keep in touch but never did until 1983 when a telephone call while I was on the Leader news desk renewed my links with him.

The caller told me that Mike was fighting for his life in a Cardiff hospital after he was tackled while playing rugby for Llantrisant RFC which resulted in his rib cage crushing his heart.

While being driven by ambulance from the rugby ground Mike "died" twice and it needed frantic efforts to keep him alive.

For weeks Mike hovered between life and death before returning to his Llantrisant home where he would wait for the only thing that could save his life-a new heart.

During the weeks Mike was waiting for a heart transplant I visited him at his Llantrisant home and was shocked to see how ill he was.

But even though his appearance had changed dramatically there was one feature still very evident-the old defiant smile.

Mike did get the call to go to Harefield hospital where he successfully came through a heart transplant operation and I was among the crowds of people who welcomed him home in August 1983.

When all the media interest had subdued and the last of the well wishers had gone I sat down with Mike and he told me the effects of being a heart plant recipient.

He said:"I have to come to grips with it mentally as well as physically".

"I am afraid".

"If I wake up in the middle of the night and so much as have a hiccup my mind goes into a turmoil thinking my new heart is about to pack in."

Mike lived each day as if it was to be his last.

He was often making the headlines including when working for Tesco stores he chased a shoplifter for half a mile before catching him.

Our next meeting was in Porthcawl where I saw Mike sitting outside a public house.

He looked tanned and fit.

"Are you taking it easy?" I asked him.

"Come on Dave," he replied,"I told you I would never sit in an armchair and watch the world go by.

That's not my style."
It couldn't last however and six years on his new heart began to have major problems which resulted in yet another heart transplant at Harefield.
Within weeks of receiving his second heart I saw him at a rugby match supporting his beloved Llantrisant club.
He looked very ill but the confidence was still there.
"I'm on my way back," he told me,"you had better believe it"
Three weeks before his death I visited him at his home in Llantrisant.
He was clearly unwell and told me that he was waiting for extensive tests at Harefield Hospital.
"I have no regrets." he said,"not even against playing rugby. It was something that just happened.
"No-one is to blame."
For the first time I detected a note of resignation in Mike's manner and it worried me.
This wasn't the Mike Ward I had come to know.
"Look Dave whatever will be will be".
"I don't know what the future holds for me but I know I can't control it."
We spoke of the possibility of him receiving a third heart and he told me there might be a chance it would happen.
"I've lived my life the way I wanted to live it.
"I wouldn't have it any other way".
"My family have been wonderful to me and I have met many, many special people during the last eight years".
"If I could have one wish granted it would be to play a game of rugby again".
And then came the dreaded phone call to tell me that he had died.

Mike Ward's supreme battle for life ended in the early hours of the morning when his second heart collapsed after he got up from bed to go to the bathroom.

The doctor said afterwards that 36-year-old Mike had died instantly "As if someone had suddenly switched off a light."

The pal who I used to call "the hell raiser with the film star looks" is no more and I miss him more than words on this page can say.

I have treasured memories of the time we worked together in the warehouse.

Over the years I penned countless words about my pal- these were my last.

"Many people loved you for what you were Mike and I was one of them.

I will cherish his smile and what he gave to people along the way.

Goodbye Mike and God Bless.

I DID IT MY DOWN YOUR WAY.

IN 1983 the editor came up with the bright idea of running a series of features called "Down Your Way".

I reckon he must have been a fan of the popular BBC radio series called "Down Your Way" which ran from 1946 to 1992, originally on the Home Service, later on BBC Radio 4. It was usually broadcast on Sunday afternoons and involved a presenter visiting towns around the United Kingdom, to chat to residents.

I remember I used to listen to it in the 1960s when Franklin Engelmann was the presenter.

"Down Your Way" came my writing way one rainy Friday afternoon when myself and a photographer were desptached to Evanstown, a suburb of Gilfach Goch, to interview residents and take some pictures.

When we arrived we parked the car opposite the Evanstown Social Club.

We sat and we waited and the only thing that passed by was one man and his dog.

I got a bit worried because I needed to talk to enough people to make a full page spread.

It was a matter of write or bust so me and the photographer decided that the only way we could get some comments and pics was from inside the club.

When we set foot through the front door a sea of frowned faces swung our way.

In the silence the card playing stopped in mid deal and pint glasses were set firmly down on tables, the only thing missing was someone playing the piano.

I felt like Marshal Dillon going in after the bad guys.

We were the strange strangers in town.

When we got to the bar and asked for drinks the bartender gave us a long hard look and asked: "Nothing to do with the Dole are you?"

"Er ..No.."

"Anything to do with VAT?"

"No.Listen I'm a reporter and this is the photographer".

"We are from the Llantrisant Observer and we are here to have a chat about the community."

"Hey boys," shouted the bartender,"It's alright this pair are from the Llantrisant Observer".

That was the signal for a happy writing hour.

I'M GLAD I KNEW CLIVE.

SOMETIMES when you try and re-unite with an old work colleague it does not end in happy circumstances as I found out in 2016.

While trying to search for a reporter pal named Clive Dennier this is what I discovered.

Liverpool born Clive, who was a reporter for the Rhondda Leader and Pontypridd Observer in the 1980s, died after he went for a walk and fell while crossing a river in the Scottish Highlands.

A post mortem later stated that Clive, who was aged 50, died from a head injury and drowning following his fall.

It was while working for the Strathspey and Badenoch Herald newspaper that Clive was reported missing when he failed to go into work.

Coastguard, Mountain Rescue and helicopters were deployed and his body was eventually found after he had been missing for 10 weeks.

After leaving the Welsh Harp based office Clive went on to working for the Eastern Daily Press, in Norfolk, the Gulf Daily News in Bahrain before moving to the Scottish Highlands.

Following his death Clive was named as the recipient of the Barron Trophy, recognising his lifetime achievement in journalism.

In his memory the CLIVE campaign (Climbers Location and Identification Verification Envelope) has also been set up which encourages those taking to the hills to write details of their excursion and then leave them in an envelope with a responsible person.

I have lovely memories of Clive. He may have been a Scouser but he was passionate about the Rhondda.
He was a first class reporter and I will never forget him.

TOMMY THE LORD OF THE RINGS.

I was among 200 people who attended the funeral of valley boxing legend Tommy Farr in March 1986.

The funeral service of Clydach born Tommy took place in St Andrew's Church, Tonypandy.

The hard men of boxing's past paid homage to a man who was one of life's champions.

On 30 August 1937, Tommy fought world heavyweight champion Joe Louis at the height of his career at Yankee Stadium, New York City.

He gained much respect despite losing a controversial points decision after 15 rounds.

Louis, one of the greatest heavyweights of all time, had knocked out 8 of his previous 9 opponents and proceeded to knock out his next 7, but was fearlessly attacked and hurt by Farr.

The 50,000 crowd booed when Louis was awarded the decision after referee Arthur Donovan, Sr. had seemingly raised Farr's glove in victory.

Tonypandy town hall was opened in the middle of the night so the community could listen to it together, but so many turned up that they had to rig extra speakers outside.

Boxing greats including Jack Petersen, Eddie Thomas, Glen Moody, Howard Winstone and Sid Worgan fondly remembered the life of Thomas George Farr the tough kid from Clydach who blossomed into a gentle giant to become the idol of Welsh boxing.

Tommy's widow Carol "Monty" Farr, son Richard and daughter in law Jeanette heard Rhondda Mayor Glyn James speak passionately of a man he said had become part of Rhondda' heritage.

He added:"Tommy Farr was truly lord of the rings. He was full of confidence, had great stickability and glowed with charisma."

The service was conducted by the Reverend Stephen Ryan,Rural Dean of Rhondda and a tribute was also given by Ieuan James Owen the Presbyterian Minister of Treforest.

Before Tommy's final journey to Trealaw cemetery the Cambrian Male Voice choir sang his favourite hymns.

People stood in tribute along Dunraven Street,Tonypandy, as the procession made the short Journey to Trealaw Cemetery where Tommy's ashes were laid to rest in the same grave as his parents under the marble monument with the inscription "In death reunited."

CHAPTER 4
WAY UP NORTH

IN 1986 I pocketed my pen and pad and headed North to Lancashire.

I had taken up the offer of a job as a sub editor for a newspaper called The Citizen.

The Citizen was a free weekly newspaper distributed to communities in Lancashire including Burnley, Preston. Clitheroe, Chorley and the head office in Blackburn where I was based.

I was like a fish out of the River Rhondda on that subs desk. The chief sub editor was a guy called Dave Miller who I had a lot of respect for.

Dave would report on football matches on a Saturday and whenever there was a match involving a Welsh side there was one word which always puzzled him.

"What does the Welsh word 'dim' mean?" he asked.

"Whenever there is a Welsh speaking bloke commentating on the game it is always 'dim this' and 'dim that."

"It means nothing Dave," I said.

"Nothing?"

"Yeah nothing, nil, zero or as you say in these parts Nowt."

There are two not so memorable moments I can recall during my reporting life with the Citizen.

A reporter who was supposed to be a guest at businessmens' golf dinner/presentation was unable to go and I was not so much asked but told by the managing director that I would have to replace him.

I could sense trouble ahead because what I knew about golf you could write on a tee.

I ended up sitting down at a very plush do with a bunch of high flying businessmen who lived and breathed golf.
"What am I doing here?" I thought.
When the feast was finished the golf club gaffer came over to me and asked:"Have you prepared your speech?"
"Speech?What speech?"
He said as a representative of the Citizen I had to go out in front of a packed hall of golf fanatics and give a speech.
Oh No!
And so I ended being introduced to a packed audience not knowing what to prattle on about.
Okay so I forgot the golf and what turned out to be a stunned silence I reeled off a rugby story.
Must have been the shortest speech they ever heard.
The other occasion was when I was invited to a Sports Evening at Turf Moor, the home of Burnley Football Club.
I was sat next to former Northern Ireland footballer Jimmy McIlroy who played almost 500 matches in Burnley colours.
There were a few guest speakers but the not so stand out one for me was a former England rugby international who did nothing but put the boot in anything to do with Welsh rugby.
Jimmy had a big grin on his face when he said:"Relax Taff. No matter what he is saying you are among friends here."
It was a long night.

JUST MY IMAGINATION

While working on the subs desk at The Citizen newspaper Dave Miller told me that The Sunday Sport were looking for people to work on Saturday afternoons putting together sports pages.

Sunday Sport, a tabloid newspaper, was established in 1986 and is known for carrying ludicrous stories, such as "London Bus Found Frozen In Antarctic Ice", "World War II Bomber Found On The Moon" and "Woman Gives Birth To 8lb Duck".
The newspaper had a team of part time editorial staff based in the Lancashire Evening Telegraph office in Blackburn.
"Why don't you give it a try?" said Miller.
I did give it a try and found myself having an interview with a no nonsense Cockney editor.
"Have you read Sunday Sport?" he demanded.
"Of course," I answered.
"Then you will know what this newspaper is all about. I am not concerned about reporters writing the truth".
"The ones I need have to have vivid imaginations".
"Do you reckon you will fit the bill?"
"Sure I can".
"Okay I will try you out on a shift on Saturday. If you do alright I will keep you on if not then you will be out."
When Saturday came I was pointed to a desk and told that I needed to put together a 400 words piece about the First Division (later to become the Premier Division) matches for the newspaper's Scottish edition.
It meant that at half time I had to phone correspondents, mostly former football players, to get a rundown on what was happening at the matches they were at.
Looking back I think it was a correspondent at Maine Road, the home of Manchester City that I happened to telephone call.

"It's 0-0," my contact said," nothing much to report really except for a bit of crowd trouble involving a few people which the stewards quickly sorted out."
And so I added it to my report.
It was just then that the editor looked over my shoulder at my report on the computer screen.
"What's that about crowd trouble?" he asked.
"Nothing much," I said," just thought I'd mention it in my report."
"Change it to a riot," he said.
"No!.No!.It's not a riot."
"Did you hear me-change it to a riot."
While working there I got friendly with a young reporter called Tony Livesey.
Tony, who lived in Burnley, would give me a lift to and from my Saturday afternoon shift in Blackburn.
After finishing one Saturday shift Tony told me he had been offered a full time reporting job at the Sunday Sport's head office.
"Why don't you come and join me?" he asked.
It was an offer I more than positively refused.
Tony went on to spend a highly successful career with the Daily Sport and Sunday Sport as an editor-in-chief and managing director and also as radio broadcaster.
My time working with the Sunday Sport was something I'll never forget.
There used to be a saying in the newspaper game that if you wanted to read the truth then buy a Quality Street newspaper such as the Times, Telegraph or Independent.

If you are not fussy about the truth and just like reading incredible stories then get the "Red Tops" such as The Sun, The Mirror or the Daily Star.
I don't know what category the Sunday Sport would be in.
WHEN THE BOAT GOES OUT.
AT the back end of the 1980s I could still not shake off being a roving reporter.
It was while I was working for a newspaper in Lancashire that a reporting job being advertised in Scotland caught my weak eye.
The job was with a newspaper called the Campbeltown Courier and I was attracted by the decent pay and perhaps free haggis.
Campbeltown I discovered was situated on the beautiful peninsula of Kintyre and was once proclaimed 'the whisky capital of the world' which didn't mean a lot to a shandy drinking man like me.
Anyway I was invited north of the border for an interview which took place in Oban.
After settling back on a tartan couch the managing director described all the reporting tasks that needed to be done.
"Campbeltown is a very close, very parochial community," he said.
"No problem for a Nantymoel native like me," I thought.
"Canna you take photographs?" he asked.
Well I did say yes because I had a box brownie which I put to good use on holiday in Ogmore by Sea.
"Because you see laddie not only will you have to write stories but you will have to take photographs as well."
Righto!

"Not only that," he said,"but twice a week you will have to take a boat across to the island to get stories from there."
Boat?
I hope he didn't mean rowing a boat.The last boat I was on was on the kiddies ride in Trecco Bay fairground.
Island?
Barry Island was my limit.
Guess what?
I didn't get the job.

IN THE EYE OF THE BEHOLDER.

IN 1988 I quit my reporting job in Lancashire and took up an offer to be a scribe on a newspaper which was being launched in West Wales.

The newspaper was called the Swansea Gazette and to give the launch some impact someone came up with the bright idea of holding a beauty contest.

And so it was down to me to run a story asking Swansea's most beautiful young women to put their names forward to be crowned Miss Swansea Gazette.

It was arranged for all those interested to attend a pub on a Friday night where myself and the promotions manager would meet up with them.

When I walked into the pub and saw the half a dozen women there I made a quick exit.

Believe me it was no beauty parlour.

When the promotions manager poked his head into the room he made a faster exit than me.

"We have to get some attractive women for this contest," he said,"tell you what, I'm going to pop into the bar for a drink but I want you to go outside and if you see any pretty young things walking along the road ask them if they would like to take part in a beauty contest."

"Yeah sure", I thought,"I fancy going out onto the Kingsway at 8 o'clock on a Friday night asking young women if they would like to enter a beauty contest but what I didn't fancy was spending a night in a cell in Swansea Central police station."

Anyway slowly we managed to get some wannabee beauty queens to come forward.

And then there was the morning that I was called to the office reception to meet two young women.

One wanted to enter the beauty contest and had brought her friend along with her.

I invited them into my office and took down some details.

The young woman gave me her name and address and her age which was 18.

"Could you tell me your vital statistics?" I asked.

"You wha..?" she asked with a glazed look.

"I need to know your vital statistics," I said.

"What's he on about?" she asked turning to her friend.

"He wants to know how big your bust is," she said.

Somebody save me!!!

COUGH UP OR ELSE.

I'LL never forget the day a front page story almost landed me in a prison cell.

It happened around 30 years ago when Cardiff City football club were set to play Swansea at the Vetch field and it goes without me saying that then, as now, there is no love lost between the Bluebirds and the Swans.

Football hooliganism was all the rage at that time and my editor came up with the bright idea to for me to do an interview with some Swansea football hooligans to find out what they had planned for the visiting Cardiff fans.

I did have reservations about doing the story but I made a few phone calls and managed to arrange a meeting with six of the hooligans in secret in a Swansea pub.

They told me things like how they planned to ambush Cardiff fans among other methods of attack they had under wraps.

When I had finished chatting to them the leader of the gang warned me that "if any of them were identified from the story in the newspaper they knew where to find me."

So I filed the story which appeared in the Thursday morning edition two days prior to the match.

Within an hour of the newspaper hitting the Swansea streets the editor received a telephone call.

The caller said that the editor and I needed to go to Swansea Central police station immediately.

When we arrived there we were ushered into an office where a stern faced police chief sat at a desk which had the Swansea Gazette and my story on it.

And he let us have it both barrels.

"Do you realise the damage this story can cause?" he growled.

"We have to deal with enough trouble which might occur between fans on Saturday without this," he said jabbing his finger at my story.

"This is incitement," he said.

Back then incitement which the law said: "consisted of persuading, encouraging, instigating, pressuring, or threatening so as to cause another to commit a crime" was an offence.

"Now," said the police chief fixing his eyes firmly on me,"I want you to name names.
Who are these people? Where did you meet them?"
"Sorry sir but I can't do that."
"You realise," said he,"that I can have you both put in a cell because of this."
"Sorry but I am still not telling you anything."
It was with a lot of relief when he finally waved his hand and said "Go".
The upshot was that there was a lot of running battles between the supporters after the match.
But that is one story I didn't do.

GRAND CALL FOR CATHERINE.

I remember one particular day when I had a phone call from a lady asking if I would like to interview her daughter who was a dancer and an aspiring actress.
She said her daughter's name was Catherine Zeta Jones and I could do the interview at the Grand Theatre in Swansea where she was rehearsing.
I took up the offer and when I arrived at the Grand Catherine was there with another young singer named Ria Jones.
Little did I know then that I was chatting to two young women who were set for brilliant careers in the world of entertainment.
Catherine became a Hollywood star and married a certain Mr Douglas while Ria has become an internationally renowned West End star of the highest calibre having performed in leading roles in numerous West End musicals.
But that wasn't the last story I did about Catherine Zeta Jones.

In 1991 the 22-year-old Catherine, who was starring in the TV series "The Darling Buds of May", visited the Rhondda to keep a promise to her uncle.
Catherine called in to Treherbert Methodist Church to present a £4,000 cheque to Brian Davies of the Treherbert Ambulance station to buy essential equipment for the station.
The cash was raised by Treherbert Spar Grocers and local chemists S and C Jones.
The young star was invited to the valley by her great uncle Cecil Pritchard who helped organise the event.
Mr Pritchard said at the time that Catherine was a "lovely girl who willingly signed autographs."
It was a lovely gesture.

AN INTERVIEW WITH BOBBY'S GIRL.

I fell in love with Susan Maughan back in 1962 even though she wanted to be "Bobby's Girl".
 And I had the chance to meet the love of my teenage life.
A pantomime called "Goldilocks and the Three Bears" was set to delight the audiences at the Grand Theatre.
There was a pre panto evening arranged in which the Press and other local bigwigs were asked to attend.
When I saw Susan was among the cast I jumped at the chance.
I did get an interview with cast members including John Inman of "Are You Being Served" fame among others but my wandering left eye was always on the lookout for Susan.
And then I spotted her.
I downed a couple of double shandies and cleaned my glasses ready to make my move.

I puffed my chest out and swaggered across the floor trying my best to be the ace reporter I was not.

"Hi Susan" I said, my "name is David Edwards and I am a reporter with the Swansea Gazette. I wonder if I could have an interview."

"I'd be delighted," she smiled.

I had only just got my best biro out of my top pocket when a so called "friend" of mine who knew the history between me and Susan decided to butt in.

"Hi Susan," he said,"did you know Dave has always been stars-truck over you".

"You will make him the happiest man in Swansea if you give him your autograph". I wanted the Grand floor to open up and swallow me.

WHEN LENNY GOT THE BOOT.

AMONG those taking panto part was ventriloquist Terry Hall and his popular puppet Lenny the Lion.

Towards the end of the night myself and a photographer along with Terry and Lenny kept company at the bar.

Come closing time I think I must have had too many double shandies because I kept calling Terry "Lenny" and the lion "Terry".

When it came time to go home Terry said he would have to call a taxi because he was staying in a hotel in the Mumbles.

The photographer said: "There's no need. I am going that way.I'll give you a lift".

My lasting memory was of the photographer opening the boot of his car and Terry hurling poor Lenny inside.

Those double shandies must have really kicked in because I felt sorry for Lenny whose catchphrase was:"Aw, don't embawass me."

Terry created Lenny the Lion in 1954 after he visited the zoo while working at the summer season in Blackpool.

Lenny was made from an old fox fur and papier-mâché, with a golf ball for the nose.

Sadly Terry Hall died in 2007.

I'm not sure what happened to Lenny.

A Grand memory.

BONDING WITH DOROTHY.

I was once contacted by a radio DJ pal who said that singer Dorothy Squires was visiting the Swansea Sound Studio and would I like to meet her for an interview.

"Would love to, " said me.

When I arrived at the studio I was warned to "tread lightly" because the Pontyberem born singer could be "a bit fiery".

I knew she had a hatred of the Press but I had a lovely interview with her.

I didn't know what I was in for when Dorothy flounced into the studio but it turned out to be an enjoyable interview.

Mind you she swore like a trooper and literally cried on my shoulder about the breakdown of her relationship with Bond star and ex husband Roger Moore.

It was a pleasant hour in her company and when I finally pocketed pen and notebook she asked:"Where are you going now?"

"Back to the office," I said.

"Forget the office," said she,"Let's go down the market and have some faggots and peas."

I'm afraid the office won.

Years later I thought I would be in with a chance to interview Dorothy again when the singer had hit very hard times and was given a Trebanog home to live in by her faithful friend Esme Cole.
I contacted Esme to ask Dorothy if I could meet up with her again and also mention the Swansea interview.
Esme later rang me and said: "Sorry Dave I did ask Dorothy but she said:'No way. I've never heard of him."
From her many songs my favourite is one called "Maman" from the musical Mata Hari.
The song is about the irony of war and is well worth listening to on You Tube or whatever.
Dorothy died in Llwynypia hospital in 1998 aged 83 while her dear friend and biggest fan Esme Cole died in 2017.
:
:

CHAPTER 5
MEETING "NORMAN BATES".

AFTER putting my full stop to my final Swansea Gazette story I decided once again to take up residence in the Rhondda.

Another decision I made was to move away from newspaper reporting and throw in my writing lot into public relations.

I soon realised I had made a career mistake.

I just didn't get the writing challenges I needed.

For example one of my typing tasks was writing a 1,000 word advertising feature for a factory making steel pipes.

When I had completed the feature it was scrutinised the factory's owner who would make changes which I didn't really agree with.

Don't get me wrong the trappings were there-a company car and a good wage but it just wasn't for me.

So I packed in PR and decided to join a press agency.

It was different and challenging which was important for me.

A press agency is about generating stories that would be of interest to the media.

I did a lot of sentences at Cardiff Crown Court where I would move from court room to court room to try and pick up the best stories.

When I did get a good story I would head to the nearest payphone to ring over the report to the office and they would put it "on the wire."

When I saw Anthony Perkins in the film "Psycho" in the picture house in Nantymoel Workmens Hall in 1960 I never dreamt I would see him in the flesh almost thirty years later walking into Cardiff Magistrates Court.

It was early one morning in 1989 while working for the Agency that I received a telephone call to say that "Norman Bates" was on his way to face Cardiff Magistrates .
"Norman Bates" was in reality renowned actor Anthony Perkins who was the star of Alfred Hitchcock's blockbusting film "Psycho" and he also starred in the 1956 movie "Friendly Persuasion".
And so it came to reporting pass that myself and a photographer got over to Cardiff Magistrates Court just in time to see Mr Perkins going inside.
The Oscar nominated New York born star, who found fame playing the deranged Norman Bates in "Psycho", had been arrested on a drugs charge while staying at a hotel in Cardiff while filming for a TV channel.
Before leaving the States the 57-year-old star decided to wrap a small amount of cannabis and post it to his Cardiff address.
However the package arrived before he managed to check into the hotel and was mistakenly given to somebody else called Mr Perkins who was a guest there.
The guest informed the hotel management who contacted the police.
In court Perkins, who died in 1992, admitted to being "deeply embarrassed" by the offence of illegally importing 1.3g of cannabis with a street value of just £4.50, enough to make up no more than six cigarettes' worth and was fined £200.
Never got do to an interview-even though I tried some "friendly persuasion."

A MEAL WITH ALEXANDER.

Alexander Cordell is one of my favourite authors so it was quite a thrill for me to sit down and have a meal with him and his lovely wife Donnie many years ago.

While at the Agency I attended a presentation at a hotel in Cardiff Bay I was sat next to the couple and what a delightful experience it was.

When Alexander discovered I was from the Rhondda he was intrigued about everything that was happening in the valley.

I could sense that they were a very devoted couple.

Alexander penned some remarkable books including the Rape of the Fair Country, The Hosts of Rebecca and This Sweet and Bitter Earth which focused on the Tonypandy Riots.

The death of his beloved wife Donnie affected Alexander greatly and in November 1997 he died of a heart attack while walking near the Horseshoe Pass in Denbighshire.

He is buried at Llanfoist, Abergavenny

Lovely memories of a lovely couple.

RADIO TIMES WITH MAX.

I won't forget my "Radio Times" with Max Boyce.

One particular day the boss at the press agency I worked for said he needed me to cover a rugby match in Glynneath.

He told me it was the usual copy for the Echo, Mail and what have you but also a radio summary for Swansea Sound.

He said: "It's just a one minute match update at half time and then a one minute summary at full time."

"Hang on," said me,"I may get away with the written word but not with the spoken word. I've never done radio before."

"You'll be fine," said he.
And so I reluctantly arrived at the Glynneath rugby ground well before kick off.
Mobile phones were a thing of the distant future so I had to find a telephone somewhere.
The club secretary said: "There's a phone here in the clubhouse. You are welcome to use that."
With half time approaching I wended my way to the clubhouse and nervously made the call to Swansea Sound.
The programme producer said: "Give me a few minutes Dave and then I'll be ready for your report."
Suddenly another voice came on the phone line.
"Can I speak to Dai please?" said voice.
"Can you get off the line please?" said a panic stricken me.
Seconds later another voice came over the phone:"Is the doctor there?"
Oh No!
The next voice was that of the producer:"Okay Dave I'll count down from ten then go ahead and do your summary."
"Hold it.You can't.There's a crossed line here."
"Can you find another phone quickly?" he asked..
Thank goodness the next voice I heard was from Max Boyce who was behind the bar.
"Everything alright?" he asked.
When I explained my dialling dilemma he led me outside the club and pointed to a house across the way.
"Go to that house and tell the lady who answers the door that Max sent you to use the phone."
The door was opened by a lovely elderly lady who pulled up a chair and not only gave me the phone but a cup of tea and a cake as well.

I did manage to do both my match summaries although a crossed line nearly killed the budding radio star.
I never did get the chance to thank Max.

THE CLAIRVOYANT AND A PUNCTURE.

WHILE working for the Agency I got a call from an old reporting pal of mine who together with a couple of partners were planning to launch a free newspaper called "News of the Valleys."

Based in an office in Aberdare the newspaper's aims was to carry stories linked to the Rhondda, Taff Ely and Cynon Valley.

It was in direct competition with Celtic Press so it was going to be a tough editorial call but I took the job.

It was there that this happened.

My office phone rings.

Voice at the other end: "Wanna good story?"

Now where have I heard that before.

Voice:"I'm a clairvoyant."

"Oh Yeah."

Voice: "I predicted Kennedy's assassination and Elvis' death."

"Never".

Voice:" I can tell you what is going to happen in the future and some of it is 'orrible."

"Really".

Voice:"Can I pop into see you tomorrow morning?"

"Well it is coming up to deadline but if you can make it about 10.30 we can have a chat then."

Voice:"See you then".

The following morning 10.30 came and went and the clairvoyant eventually turned up around noon.

"Sorry I'm late," he said,"my car had a puncture."
And he's a clairvoyant!.
An then after the interview had finished he said:"Which is the way out?"
Some clairvoyant!.
You couldn't make it up.
And on another telephone call time...
Voice: "I need you to put my story in the newspaper."
"What's the problem?"
Voice:"I've got agorophobia and nobody will listen to me. I can't get any benefits and I'm at the end of my tether.
"I haven't put a foot outside my house for more than a year.Thank goodness I've got my wife to help me"
"Okay. I will give you a call when I am next up the Rhondda and I'll see what I can do to help."
A few days later I had a job up the Rhondda so I thought I would give him a call.
A woman answered the phone.
"Can I speak to your husband?" I asked.
"I'm sorry he's not here at the moment.He won't be long he's just popped down the shop for some fags."
Only in the Rhondda!
I had an enjoyable reporting period with the News of the Valleys but sadly it didn't last.
Beside myself there was an editor, and two young reporters gathering the valley news.
I knew my reporting time was up when I arrived back from a job to an empty office.
I was a one man reporting band-the paper was more or less doomed.

It kept going for a couple of weeks more before the final edition was printed.

It looked as if the first time in my life that I would be out of a job.

CHALLENGING TIMES.

All was not lost however because one of the advertising girls had landed a job with a newly launched free newspaper based in Caerphilly called the "The Challenger."

The Challenger's owner was keen to take on an editor and wanted to know if I was interested.

I needed a job it was that simple.

The Challenger had plenty of adverts and not a lot of editorial which was something I was not used to.

The staff were a great bunch of people to work with but I was always on the lookout for greener reporting pastures.

I realised that I couldn't dare challenge the Challenger when things came to a head on the front page on one particular edition.

I had a great story planned for the front page. It was a scoop and I needed to get it in print as soon as possible.

Trouble was brewing however when a rep had sold advertising space on the promise that the blurb and a picture would go on the front page.

I was lost for words.

"It can't be done," I told the rep,"the front page is for news not for an advert."

"We'll see about that," he responded," I'll go and see the boss."

The owner came to see me and said:"Sorry but the ad goes on the front page."

"You mean you are going to sacrifice a red hot story on the front page for advertising space."
"I'm afraid so. It is revenue and that comes before news."
With the boss having the last front page word I knew then that my time with the Challenger was up.

RUBY AT THE LITTLE THEATRE.

I THEN discovered that there was another free newspaper going to be launched in Caerphilly.
The Caerphilly Chronicle was part of the Celtic Press Group and aimed at gathering news throughout the Caerphilly borough.
I was a one reporting band at the Caerphilly based Newspaper and I enjoyed my time there.
It was while I was there that I had a phone call asking me if I would like to interview singer Ruby Murray who was going to perform at the Little Theatre in Blackwood.
In the 1950s, Ruby had a smash hit with the song "Softly Softly" had her own television show, starred at the London Palladium, appeared in a Royal Command Performance and toured the world.
The Little Theatre is a converted Methodist chapel which has been in use as a theatre constantly since 1956.
Belfast born Ruby Murray was not in the best of health when I did that interview with her in 1991.
During our chat she said: "I have performed many times at the London Palladium, including the Royal Variety Performance but I have never been so nervous as I am of going out onto that stage."
Ruby needn't have worried.
She proved what a fabulous singing star she was and got a standing ovation.

Ruby Murray continued performing until close to the end of her life.

She died of liver cancer, aged 61, in December 1996 in Torquay after a long struggle with alcoholism.

I NEVER GOT TO SEE PARIS.

WHILE I was reporting here there and everywhere the Rhondda Leader/Pontypridd Observer office in Taff Street had moved to Dowlais where the newspapers were being printed.

A change of heart by the editorial chiefs however resulted in the office once again returning to Pontypridd this time situated in Market Street.

So after an absence of six years I was fortunate enough to return where it all started for me when I was once again offered a job as a reporter with the Rhondda Leader.

I joined a team of new reporters while my old colleague Kayrin Davies was the editor of the Rhondda Leader while Dudley Stephens still held the reporting reins at the Ponty Observer.

It was nice to be back.

I never did get any "faraway freebies" during my reporting stint with the Rhondda Leader.

While other reporters were lucky enough to be sent swanning off to Scotland or were away to Austria to cover valley linked stories the furthest I ever travelled was to Blaencwm.

But that almost changed one day when I got a call from the late, great, valley actor Brian Meadows.

Brian along with the cast of a valley based theatre group were preparing to stage their version of the hit TV show Allo' Allo'.

Brian said as part of their preparation the cast were taking a trip to Paris to take in the sights and get that "French feeling" for their show.

Brian said:"We would like to invite you to come along with us and do a story on our Paris trip."

My freebee French fantasy was stopped dead in its tracks however when I put the idea to my editor.

"When are they going on this trip?" she asked.

When I told her she said: "Sorry Dave no can do. All the sports reports come in then and you are the only one who can deal with that."

Couldn't even get some French leave.

I last saw Brian, who sadly died in 2011, at a boot sale and as usual he made a great fuss with the warmest of welcomes.

Brian will always be much missed.

I'M A DISTRACTION.

Sometimes in my reporting life I discovered that in dreadful situations there was always a glimmer of humour.

Like this for instance....

I was on the newsdesk when I had a call from a police officer about a distraction theft involving an elderly lady.

It was the usual sort of thing. Two blokes had called to her house pretending to be from the water board and while one kept her talking the other one went upstairs to steal cash and other valuables.

The police officer said that the lady wouldn't mind being interviewed as it might be a warning to others about this sort of crime.

"She is very old, lives alone and can get rather confused," he said.

And so I took up the offer and visited what turned out to be a lovely old lady who was shocked and angry about what had happened.

I enjoyed a cup of tea and a lovely chat with her and after the interview came away thinking how can people be so low as to do this sort of thing.

A couple of weeks later I was passing the lady's house so I decided to pop in and see how she was getting on.

She gave me a lovely welcome and told me to sit down and have a cup of tea.

"He came back you know," she said.

"Who came back?"

"That bloody robber," she said," the one who stole my stuff."

"Never"

"Yes," she said,"The swine sat there where you are writing stuff down on a notebook.Ugly looking sod with glasses."

It was then it dawned on me the "robber" she was talking about was ME!!

Spoilt my reporting day that did.

MISSING A FOOTBALL VAN.

IT was the year 1995 and Welsh League outfit Ton Pentre had qualified for the Intertoto Cup which featured the top football sides in Europe.

One of the games Ton played was against top class Dutch outfit Heerenveen and because Ynys Park did not meet the competition's grounds standards the match was played at Cardiff Arms Park.

Myself and a photographer were despatched to the stadium with the orders to get "plenty of action shots."

Included in the Ton side was Brett Davey, who when not kicking a round ball at Ynys Park was booting an oval ball at Sardis Road playing full back for Pontypridd.

Ton lost a very one sided match 7-0 and were soon eliminated from the competition.

The Dutch side were in total control of the match and I had a job to keep a reporting track of the subs they were sending on.

A few days later my match report and pics appeared in the Leader's sports pages.

Many moons had passed when the editor called me into his office where he held up a copy of the "News of the World" and a lead story on a sports page under a banner headline "I Played Against Van Nistelrooy."

The story was about Brett playing in the match against the Dutch striker who found football fame with Real Madrid and Manchester United.

"Remind me," said the editor,"You did cover this match didn't you?"

To this day I swear I never saw the name Van Nistelrooy on the team sheet or among the subs being sent on.

Me and the photographer went straight into the dark room to see if we did get a file picture of Van and Brett going for the ball.

In the end we found one of Brett and a player who looked like Van Nistelrooy but having said that he could have been a postman from Amsterdam who was a part time player.

There again I suppose it all could all have been "Double Dutch" to me.

CHAPTER 6

BEING A GHOST WRITER.

I'VE written a few ghost stories and I've been a ghost writer but the biggest spectre of all was when I spoke to a ghost on the phone.

It happened like this...

We ran a story in the Leader about a bloke who appeared in Crown Court to face a charge of burglary.

In his defence his solicitor told the court that his client's father had died a month before committing the burglary and that he was "in the grip of an addiction."

Anyway within an hour of the Leader hitting the valley streets I had a phone call from the "dead father".

The very much alive father said that he was not only shocked and angry with his son but also with the fact that such a lie could have been said in Crown Court.

I contacted the CPS (Crown Prosecution Service) to find out how this could have happened.

I mean after all if myself or any others had come out with such a lie in court we would have been done for perjury.

A CPS spokesman told me that the solicitor was "acting on his client's instructions" and he was perfectly entitled to make that representation.

And there was also the time...

We carried another story of a young criminal who magistrates were told by his solicitor had gone off the rails because when he was younger his parents would "lock him in the garden shed and go drinking down the club."

Following the story I was contacted by the distressed parents who I then decided to visit.

They were a decent couple with a lovely home who were devastated that their son would come out with such a blatant lie in court.

Talk about a law unto themselves.

FAGS AT FRIMLEY.

IN 1998 myself and a photographer travelled to Surrey to cover a World Darts final.

The reason we were travelling further than Blaencwm was that 31-year-old Richie Burnett from Cwmparc was stepping up to the oche against Dutchman Raymond Van Barneveld in the British Darts Organisation's World final.

The event at the Lakeside Country Club, Frimley Green, was sponsored by Embassy Cigarettes and I kid you not that when the photographer and myself walked into the Press Room fags were being thrown at us from everywhere.

I can remember the place being packed to the rafters.

It was an incredible atmosphere.

To be fair Richie wasn't short of Rhondda support as he took flight to the stage to start his attempt to regain the title he won in 1995 after defeating Dutch player Raymond Barneveld.

Between the amount of lighting, TV cameras all over the place and a baying crowd I found it incredible that the players could perform like they did.

As for the match itself it really was nerve wracking for me to watch Richie matching Barneveld in every dart throwing way in his bid to win the world title.

The match was the best of 11 sets and incredibly when it was level at 5-5 it went to a tie break with whoever winning by two legs crowned the winner.

I was biting my biro again when it got to three legs to two in favour of the Dutchman.

Burnett had had an out-shot for the title, but narrowly missed his second dart at treble 14 which would have left him on double 20.

It all ended when Barneveld hit a double eight to clinch the title.

Barneveld fell to his knees in tears while a devastated Richie stood at the side trying to take it all in.

Richie collected a runner up cheque for £20,000 while Barneveld pocketed forty grand.

When a clearly drained Richie stepped off the stage and walked into the players' room I pounced for an interview.

Big mistake.

Richie turned and gave me a disbelieving look and said:"Go away Dai" or words to that affect.

To be fair when he was fully able to compose himself a while later he did give me that interview.

BONNY WHITEHOUSE

THE Rhondda Leader's annual Bonny Babies competitions always had me reaching for the Phyllosan.

It was always more than teething problems.

There was the inevitable mix of wrong names under pictures, wrong ages and I want to forget what else.

But long before I typed a Bonny Baby's first name there was one particular bundle of joy who went from flannelette to fame.

Here's how in a story published in the Leader a few of my smiling years past.

"Valley born comedian Paul Whitehouse picked up his first sought-after award when he was just a toddler – The Baby Smile of the Rhondda.

The famed comedian was born in Stanleytown in 1958 where his dad worked for the National Coal Board and his mam was an opera singer.

But long before winning Bafta comedy awards, the London-based comedian won the popular Leader award.

In his many interviews with the Press, Mr Whitehouse, who created some of television's most memorable comedy characters – from Harry Enfield's Stavros to Irish gardener Ted in the award-winning The Fast Show – always talks about his childhood days in the valley.

He moved to London with his parents when he was four, but went back to the Rhondda Fach each summer.

He said: "I still have rose-tinted memories of wonderful times there. I can recall going on day trips to the seaside and the smell of sheep and pits.

"I always feel I should take my children back, but it would be quite a shock for them – they're little Highbury trendies.

"My mum sang with the Welsh National Opera and used to travel a bit."

He also said of the first weeks he attended a school in England: "I didn't say a word for four weeks because my Welsh accent was different to the other children.

"After a month I spoke with a London accent, but whenever I went back to Wales, I would always revert to a Welsh lilt."

Oh baby!

WAY OUT WEST WITH RON.

LOVED doing stories on a former Treorchy librarian who blazed his own writing trail by penning cowboy books.

Ron Watkins wrote several popular Black Horse Western novels despite confessing that the furthest west he had travelled was Haverfordwest.

The novels included titles such as "Stagecoach to Damnation", "Bounty Hunter's Revenge" and "A Bullet for the Preacher".

Ron, who sadly died in 2011, was a great fan of renowned Western novel author Zane Grey and whenever he had a new book published he always made sure I received a copy.

He found his inspiration to write as early as getting up at dawn to get his cowboy ideas on paper before setting off to work at a library.

It usually took him about six weeks to get a cowboy book in the publishing corral.

And it wasn't only cowboy books that he had a writing talent for.

His first novel was a suspense thriller called "Death Draws the Curtain."

Ron was born in 1930 and educated at Leominster Grammar school.

He worked as a librarian with Rhondda Borough Council rising to the position of Deputy County Librarian with Mid-Glamorgan County Council.

He was also a reader for a London publisher and President of the Bridgend Writers Circle.

As a fellow scribe I had a lot of admiration for Ron Watkins. He was a gifted writer.

SETTLING OLD SCORES.

IN 1991 I was invited to a private screening in a Cardiff Hotel of a film called Old Scores.

The made for TV film was produced by HTV Cymru Wales in association with South Pacific Pictures for the ITV Network.

The film's storyline focused on a fictional rugby match between Wales and New Zealand which was won by Wales.

On his death-bed, the touch judge confesses to failing to disallow the winning try for an infringement by the Welsh scorer.

The Welsh Rugby Union President decided that in order to set the record straight, there should be a rematch between the two teams - using the same players who had played the match 25 years earlier.

Cast members included Windsor Davies, Glyn Houston and Robert Pugh while also taking part in the film was a mixture of former Wales and New Zealand players.

These included Ian Kirkpatrick, Waka Nathan, Grahame Thorne, and Alex "Grizz" Wyllie, and Wales's Phil Bennett, Gerald Davies, Mervyn Davies, Gareth Edwards, Tony Faulkner, Dennis Hughes, Barry John, Allan Martin, David Morris, David Price, Mike Roberts, J.J. Williams, and Bobby Windsor.

I was lucky enough to meet up with Glyn Houston on a few occasions.

He was always delightful to talk to and was always very proud of his Rhondda roots.

I can't really remember how much an impact the film had when it was shown on the telly.

ON CUE WITH TERRY.

IT was a pleasure many cue balls ago to chat to a Penygraig postman who became a first class snooker player.

In 1982, at the age of 47, Rhondda born Terry Parsons chalked up the finest moment of his green baize career when he won the World Amateur Championship in Calgary, Canada.

Trailing Canadian Jim Bear 7-1 after the opening session, Parsons recovered magnificently to claim the title with an 11-8 success.

In doing so he emulated the achievements of his Welsh contemporaries Doug Mountjoy (who had won in 1976) and Cliff Wilson (1978).

When the championship was staged in Dublin Parsons attempted to retain his title.

Among the 42 players was an unknown Scottish teenager who failed to qualify from the group stages.

Fifteen years later Stephen Hendry became world professional champion.

Parsons had no trouble reaching the knockout rounds and indeed made it through to the final again.

There was to be no fairytale ending, however, and India's Omprakesh Agrawal became the first overseas player to win the title courtesy of an 11-7 triumph.

The same year, Parsons won the last of his five Welsh amateur titles, some 23 years after his first success in 1961.

"He was one of the best, authentic amateurs of the last 30 years," said Clive Everton, a fellow Welshman.

Both Everton and Terry Griffiths, the 1979 world professional champion from Llanelli, agree that Parsons could have made a decent living had he opted to rescind his amateur status.

A family and very modest man, Parsons disliked being away from the community where he spent all his life.

He combined delivering snooker breaks with letters when he was a postman and would rise at 4am before finishing his round at noon.

He managed to snatch a few hours sleep before practising on the snooker table at the Penygraig Labour Club.

"The life style wouldn't have suited Terry," added Everton.

"He was dreadfully homesick in Calgary and that was when he was winning. But there's no doubt he could have competed on the professional circuit.

"He had a solid all-round game and was an excellent match player."

Sadly Terry passed away in May 1999.

It was only once that I interviewed Terry Parsons and he was one of the nicest unassuming men I could wish to meet.

WHEN IT WAS "CURTAINS UP."

OVER the reporting years I did my share of "write ups" about shows staged by the valley's theatrical societies.

I always felt a bit of a fraud really because after all the only time I had a part on the stage was in a St David's Day play in my schooldays in Nantymoel.

Of course it was always the first night that I took my seat at the Park and Dare theatre and now and again things did go wrong.

I remember a performance called "Gypsy" based on the musical and film about the famous striptease artist Gypsy Rose Lee.

If my 73-year-old memory serves me right there was a scene where a couple were sat at a table listening to a wireless set which had a recording of Gypsy singing.
When the act stopped however the singing didn't because whoever was operating the behind the scenes tape recording of Gypsy's voice had forgotten to turn it off.
Gypsy kept singing and singing and singing........
Then there was a performance of Cinderella.
It was the scene of the Ball when everyone was awaiting the arrival of the Prince.
Suddenly somebody shouted: "Here comes the Prince."
No sign of the Prince.
Another shout:"The Prince is coming."
Still no sign of the Prince.
One more shout:"The Prince really is coming".
It was charming when the Prince did eventually turn up
Seriously though I was always in awe of the performances put on.
I could never do a bad write up.
I thoroughly enjoyed them all.

A NIGHT OUT WITH ROY.

FORMER Wales internationals Roy Paul and Swansea born Ivor Allchurch shared a few shandies when they met at a sports presentation event in the valley.
I once lived a free kick away from the Manchester City player's house in Gelli and one time down the soccer years I accompanied him to a special occasion in Cardiff.
I had a telephone call from my good friend and freelance journalist Jack Trembath asking if I could give Roy a lift to a bit of a do in a Cardiff hotel to honour Jimmy Scoular.

I was living in Gelli at the time and Roy lived a short distance away.
Former Scotland international and Newcastle player Scoular, who also managed Cardiff City FC, was the guest of honour at the function which included a host of former players as well as members of the Press.
When we arrived at the hotel, which was rather posh, Roy said he wanted to get a drink in the foyer before going up to the main reception.
After he was served a drink he noticed that the bartender had given him change for a fiver instead of a tenner.
Roy give him a look that would have frightened many of his football opponents before saying:"I maybe from the valleys but I'm not stupid."
That was Roy.
When we arrived in the main function there was only one person that everybody wanted to talk to.
And that was Roy Paul.
I have great memories of him.

A GEORDIE'S VALLEY ANTHEM.

IN 2013 I decided to do a story about the singer David Alexander and the song known as the valley anthem "If I Could See The Rhondda One More Time."
And I got quite a surprise.
I always thought that whoever penned the words to the song would have been someone who was probably born and bred in the valley.
I couldn't have been more wrong.
The words were written by a Geordie.

Johnny Caesar, who hails from South Shields, wrote the words to the popular song in 1968 while sitting in a pal's house in Quakers Yard.

He said: "I have always had a great romance with the Rhondda and it took me just 20 minutes to pen the lyrics for "If I Could See The Rhondda One More Time."

In 2013 Mr Caesar, who also played the part of Seth Armstrong's sidekick Bill Middleton in the ITV soap "Emmerdale", produced a 12-track CD called "Back to the Rhondda" in collaboration with Rhondda author and former miner Bill Richards.

Mr Richards, who owned a carpet store in Tonypandy before retiring, said then: "I was planning an internet website devoted to Cambrian Colliery and I needed permission to use the song If I Could See the Rhondda One More Time which was a huge hit for David Alexander.

"I contacted David's widow Penny and she put me in touch with Johnny Caesar who wrote the words to the song which has become the valley's anthem".

Blackwood born David Alexander eventually settled in Tenerife with Penny Page, whom he had met in 1976 and married in 1981.

He enjoyed playing golf and often sang in bars and clubs in and around Tenerife.

In November 1994 the popular singer was rushed into hospital and diagnosed with cardiomegaly (an enlarged heart) and was advised by doctors to limit his workload.

In February 1995, he suffered a heart attack and died, he was 66 years of age.

CAREY AND MICHAEL CAINE.

IN 2017 I lost a loyal friend in Carey Williams.

I first met Carey when we both worked in the TC Jones factory in Treorchy.

We had great fun there especially working night shifts. Often we would walk out into the yard outside the factory and watch the dawn break over Treorchy.

Carey, who lived in Penrhys for many years, left me with some wonderful memories.

Here's one of them...

I was on the Rhondda Leader newsdesk when I got a phone call from Carey to tell me that his daughter Alison's partner Mike had spotted film star Michael Caine walking near Penrhys golf course.

"Are you sure Carey?"

"Positive Dave. If you and a photographer get up here quickly you will have a great story."

Now something in the back of my mind told me that there might be a connection through a woman living in Penrhys who was a distant relative of the star's wife.

Eventually a not too convinced editor despatched myself and a photographer to the dizzy heights of Penrhys to hunt down Michael Caine.

We never found him.

Never even saw a Michael Caine lookalike.

I found out later he was filming on location somewhere outside the UK.

Took a long time to live that down with the other reporters.

I will never forget the Saturday nights I spent at Pentre Labour Club with Carey and his lovely wife Kitty.

Gonna miss Carey. He was a very special pal.

A LOVELY LADY CALLED RENE.

I have to mention a lovely lady called Rene Oak who was a valued correspondent for the Leader.

Rene became Leader's longest serving correspondent when she retired as a district correspondent after serving the Treherbert community for more than 30 years.

Rene from Brook Street, Blaenrhondda, was taken on as a correspondent in 1975 by the then editor John Lewis.

Blaenrhondda born Rene left the valley as a 14-year-old and found work in London.

It was there she met her husband Pete before eventually returning to the valley and settling in Brook Street.

She said: "My sister Gladys was a Treherbert correspondent before I eventually took it over.

" I needed to write an article which had to be approved by the editor before I could become a correspondent.

"I have loved every minute of being a correspondent. I have made loads of friends and I feel that I have contributed toward the community.

"It hasn't all been about hatches, matches and dispatches (births, marriages and deaths), I have also enjoyed helping in campaigns in the community.

"I have seen many changes in the valley over the years but I think the community spirit is as strong as ever.

"I have also had wonderful support from the girls who are my carers and I cannot thank them enough for all the help they give me."

Rene's husband Pete died several years ago but in 2008 she still kept in daily touch with her 97-year-old brother Frank Nation in a nursing home in Bognor.

"I have many scrapbooks of articles I have written over the years and it is lovely that I can pull them out now and again and look at them," she said.

"During the years I have served the Leader I have also seen a change of editors from John Lewis and Jim Campbell to the present one Kayrin Davies.

"I will miss doing my weekly column but I will always cherish the wonderful years that I was proud to be the correspondent of the Rhondda Leader."

"NEVILLEANGELYEO".

ALONG my reporting way there is one person I will never forget.

Neville Yeo was an indeed an amazing character.

Nev, who sadly passed away several years ago, was involved in almost every activity under the Rhondda sun.

He was a staunch member of the Acme Wheelers as well as a valley theatre group.

He was also a keen member of the Ystradyfodwg Art Society and I also believe he also found time to be a member of a computer group.

I had some magic moments with Nev, who was a very good artist.

I used to kid him by calling him NevilleangelYoe and reckoned his paintings were so good because he was a dab hand at paint by numbers.

Anyway one morning a package landed on my desk which when opened was a painting of the psychedelic gas tank in Tonypandy with my photo stuck on the side of it.

There was no indication who had sent the parcel. But I could tell by the painting style it was definitely a "NevilleangelYeo.". Great memories.

GEORGE THE MOUNTAIN STAR.

Loved doing stories about George Cole.

Not the George Cole the star of St Trinians films and Minder TV programmes but George Cole the star of the Rhigos Mountain Road.

When I was 16 years old I worked for the Ogmore and Garw District Council.

I never knew from day to day what job I would be doing. Helping the sexton in Ogmore cemetery, cutting grass, weeding pavements, painting white lines on the road, helping out on the ash cart were just some of my day to day tasks.Another one was helping a chap called Levi keep the Nantymoel side of the Bwlch mountain road free of falling rocks.

Levi had a little hut on the side of the road and every so often he would kick me out of his cabin to kick any fallen rocks off the road which may prove a danger to motorists. So I do have a sort of affinity with George Cole, from Treherbert, who more than carved his name with pride on the Rhigos mountain Road.

George had his own little "white house" on the road and of course he will always be known for his artistic qualities which he put to wonderful use when he wasn't clearing debris off the road.

George, who retired in the early 1990s, adorned the hillside with decorative flowers, windmills, miniature houses and animals which became quite an attraction for motorists using the road.

George did a great job-By any road.

CHAPTER 7
A MARILYN MONROE KISS.

"DID you know that these are the lips that kissed Marilyn Monroe?"

Those were the words that greeted me when I was introduced to singer Frankie Vaughan back in 1991.

Frankie was referring to the 1960 Hollywood film "Let's Make Love" in which he starred and shared a kiss with the Hollywood legend.

The Liverpool born singer who had hits with "Tower of Strength" and "Green Door" among others was a special guest at an event held in the Rhondda Sports Centre to honour Treorchy born World Cup football referee Clive Thomas.

Frankie and Clive had forged a friendship because of their involvement in the Boys Clubs of Wales movement.

I remember Frankie visiting a boys' club in Nantymoel back in the 1950s.

Clive at one time was President of the Boys Clubs of Wales while Frankie, who died in 1999, was an ambassador for the Movement and had visited Boys Clubs in the Rhondda as well as other parts of Wales.

Also attending the event was controversial football manager Brian Clough and singer Kenny Lynch, who had a hit with "Up on the Roof", who were also friendly with Clive.

I remember, with some trepidation approaching Brian Clough for an interview about his friendship with Clive.

"Put this in your notebook young man," he said, "Clive Thomas is the finest referee in the Football League."

And on he went.

When I was younger I idolised Marilyn Monroe.

Maybe what I should have done was given Frankie a kiss and then I could have bragged that my lips had kissed the lips of Frankie Vaughan whose lips had kissed the lips of Marilyn Monroe.

On second thoughts ...

SMILE PLEASE OWEN.

BACK in 2011 a Welsh footballing legend and a Merthyr born popular comedian joined forces to raise much needed cash for a Rhondda Boys and Girls Club.

Former Everton and Wales goalkeeper Neville Southall MBE and Owen Money MBE were the chief guests at a fundraising event held at the Treorchy Rugby Club in aid of the Treorchy Boys and Girls Club.

The event was one of several aimed at raising money to improve facilities at the Cae Mawr Field where the club's football teams play.

Club chairman Steve Williams said then: "We are hugely grateful to Neville and Owen for making it such a successful event.

"We are also indebted to our sponsors and everyone else who supported the evening."

Meeting Owen again reminded me of the time I did an interview with him when he performed at a valley club.

After the interview was done I said I needed a picture to go with the story.

The always obliging Owen told me to carry on and got in his posing position with a really big fixed smile while I got set to take the picture.

The problem was the batteries in my clapped out camera were fading fast and I couldn't get the flash to come on.

Nothing was happening and as the time was ticking away I could hear Owen muttering through a fixed smile and very clenched teeth: "Come on.Hurry up and take the damn photo."

Or words to that effect.

And then in a flash off went the flash.

I got the picture-I was never so glad to see the light.

I was never in the frame to be a photo journalist.

THE BEST LAID PLANS.

MORE often than not I managed to avoid reporting on the Local Elections count.

But I did spend many hours sat on a press bench in the Council Chamber in Pentre reporting on meetings.

It was the Rhondda Borough Council in those long gone days and I can recall some unforgettable characters arguing the toss across the chamber floor.

Providing sometimes the heated exchanges were councillors Bill Murphy, Tom Jones, Katie Rees, Mattie Collins, Geraint Davies,Dorian Rees, Gwyn Rees and John Davies among others.

And sometimes I had to bite my biro not to report all the goings on.

Like the time I was at a planning meeting when an application came up for debate for a chap who wanted to extend his garage business.

The meeting's chairman said: "Well we all know he is a bit of a Del Boy but we can still approve the application."

And often it seemed to me that the smallest issue would spark a lengthy debate.

I recall a time when there was a raging row over the Perrier water which was on tap for the councillors while they were sat in the meeting.
And at the time I didn't know what they were arguing about. When every avenue had been explored in a planning application without a decision forthcoming there was always the often used words:"We'll have a site meeting."
The Council Chamber in Pentre holds many reporting memories for me.
It was a building of character housing lots of councillor characters.
The Borough Council was abolished in 1996 to become the unitary Rhondda Cynon Taf authority.
And that meant of course the controversy of who would get top billing in the title of the new Authority.
Would it be Pontypridd, Cynon or Rhondda?.
But that's another story.

THE AMAZING GLYN JAMES.

ONE of the most remarkable characters I met during my reporting years in the valley was former Plaid Cymru councillor and Rhondda Borough Council Mayor Glyn James.
Glyn, who sadly died in 2010, was both English and Welsh speaking but after I broke bread with him at a function we both attended in the Rhondda way back when I was convinced he could also speak another language.
Following a very enjoyable meal Glyn stood up to make his mayoral speech and his opening line was:"Thank you everyone for that wonderful meal which I can only describe as gobbleupable."
"Gobbleupable?"

I couldn't find it in the dictionary.
I loved being in Glyn's company although I never knew what to expect next.
I interviewed his lovely wife Hawys following his passing and she said:"When Glyn arrived in the Rhondda at the age of 18, he started a love affair with the valley until the day he died.
"Living with Glyn was like living on the edge of a volcano.
"Whenever a challenge came along to fight a worthy cause, he channelled all his efforts into it.
"He was involved in many things and it is amazing how much he packed into his life"
He certainly did.

NOW OR NEVER FOR ELVIS.

AND what about the night I helped "Elvis" to undress?
Oh what a night that was way back in around about 1993.
The Rhondda Leader had supported a fundraising night for a local charity which was held in a Tonypandy club.
Among those who freely took to the stage was Daryl Morgan from Pentre who did a brilliant turn as Elvis Presley.
If my memory serves me right it was a sweltering hot Summer evening which proved to be a real fundraising winner.
When Elvis, I mean Daryl. had finished his act he beckoned me over to him.
"Do us a favour Dave, " he said," give me a hand to get my Elvis gear off."
Oh well!
"It's Now or Never" I thought.

I mean dressing rooms in a Rhondda workingmen's club was definitely not on the London Palladium entertainment bill so Elvis and me had to use the Gents' toilet.

Anyway I struggled to help Daryl to finally get his jump suit and boots off while getting strange looks from blokes back and fore using the toilet.

Me helping Elvis undress!

Left me proper "All Shook Up" that did.

I did a few stories about Daryl in my reporting years.

This is one of them from 2006.

"Elderly residents at a Pentre Day Centre were given a special rock 'n roll treat when 'Elvis' dropped in to give them a couple of songs.

Elvis Presley impersonator Daryl Morgan decided to give the residents at Llewellyn Day Centre in Pentre a chance to roll back the rock 'n roll years.

Daryl, said then: " I thought I'd give the residents a Christmas treat and give them a few Elvis numbers."

Centre staff member Pam Symmons said: 'The residents had a great time and many thanks to Daryl for giving us a bit of Elvis for Christmas".

JIMMY THE STARMAKER.

In 2011 Doctor Who star David Tennant was set to play the part of Rhondda-born football coach Jimmy Murphy in a film about Manchester United Football Club.

The BBC production, called United, focused on the Busby Babes, the 1958 Munich air disaster and the part played by Jimmy Murphy, known as "The Starmaker and the man about whom Sir Bobby Charlton said: "Whatever I have achieved in football, I owe to one man and only one man – Jimmy Murphy."

The year 1910 proved to be a momentous one in the Rhondda Valley.

It was the year that valley miners went into battle against pit owners in what would be marked in history as the Tonypandy Riots.

It was also a year that a bonny baby boy with an Irish name, who would become a prominent figure in one of the most famous football clubs in the world, was born in Treharne Street, Pentre.

James Patrick Murphy was brought up in a disciplined valley household in which he was taught life's values aimed at moulding him into a "decent Rhondda boy."

In later years, those values would help him achieve an important place in the colourful history of the mighty Manchester United Football Club.

A career in football was not on the agenda in the Murphy household, however, with Jimmy's parents Florence and William nurturing high hopes of him becoming a teacher.

It was with some pride that they watched their young son play the organ at a Treorchy church but the feet which pressed on the instrument pedals were itching to kick a leather football against the walls of the back streets of Pentre.

Playing football for Pentre Linnets, Pentre Boys and Treorchy Juniors, Jimmy was showing great potential in his role of inside forward.

While attending Pentre School, the footballing talent of young Murphy caught the eye of teachers Arthur Hanney and George Tewkesbury.

In later years, Jimmy would remember with great fondness the advice and encouragement given by the teachers, which would eventually win him a place in the Wales Schoolboys team.

In 1924, he represented Wales against England in Cardiff and his performance on the field came to the notice of football league outfit West Bromwich Albion.

Scouts from the Midlands based club travelled to South Wales with the aim of signing the talented Rhondda youngster.

After Jimmy's parents were given assurances that he would be well looked after, Jimmy packed a suitcase and set off to start a football career across the border.

The hustle and bustle of West Bromwich was a far cry from the younger life Jimmy had spent in the Rhondda, but although he became very homesick he was determined to become successful.

There were more honours to come for Jimmy on the national front when in 1933 at the age of 21 he became the youngest player to pull on a Wales shirt.

He remained a part of the national side for six years, during which he became the youngest player to win 21 caps and also became the Wales captain.

The highlight of the years he spent in the Midlands was playing for the Baggies in the 1935 FA Cup final against Sheffield Wednesday.

Murphy spent 11 happy years with West Brom before moving to Swindon Town in 1938, but the outbreak of World War II curtailed his club career.

Shortly after World War II was declared, most football competitions were abandoned as the country's focus turned to the War Effort.

Although his days of playing football had come to an end, Jimmy Murphy's career as a football coach was about to begin.

Jimmy was a member of the Royal Artillery which battled the enemy in the Far East and also spent four years in North Africa as a "Desert Rat."

It was a boiling hot afternoon in Bari, Italy, in 1945 and the weather matched the passionate team talk Rhondda born Jimmy Murphy was giving to a team of Army footballers. While coach Murphy was busy inspiring his team with the gusto and arm-waving of a Welsh Baptist minister, another football coach named Matt Busby listened with fascination to the Welshman's team talk.

The two coaches struck up a friendship and Busby, who would shortly return to England to become manager of Manchester United, offered Murphy a job as his assistant in the rebuilding of the war-torn club.

It was the beginning of a remarkable partnership which would endure until 1969, when the then Sir Matt Busby retired.

In his new role with United, Jimmy,together with coach Bert Whalley and chief scout Joe Armstrong, developed an exciting stream of talented young footballers who came to be known as the Busby Babes.

Jimmy was appointed the club's assistant manager in March 1955 and three years later was named as the manager of the Wales team.

On February 6, while returning to Manchester after a World Cup match between Wales and Israel in Cardiff, Jimmy heard the devastating news that the plane carrying United players, club officials and journalists home from a European

Cup match had crashed on its third attempt to take off from a slush covered runway at the Munich Riem airport.

Among the 23 who perished were eight United players, including Tommy Taylor, Roger Byrne and Duncan Edwards.

A distraught Jimmy Murphy immediately flew out to Germany and arrived in time to find relatives surrounding the bed of the gravely-ill Matt Busby who was being given the Last Rites.

Although at death's door, the United manager whispered to Jimmy, urging him "to keep the Red Flag flying".

The 47-year-old Rhondda-born coach, who played the organ in a Treorchy church as a boy, was now in charge of one of the most famous football clubs in the world, while Matt Busby battled his way back from the brink of death.

Two weeks after the Munich disaster, Jimmy managed a team which included survivors Harry Gregg and Bill Foulkes, along with seven reserves and emergency signings Ernie Taylor and Stan Crowther, in an FA Cup match in which they beat Sheffield Wednesday.

Jimmy remained as caretaker manager at Old Trafford until August, when Matt Busby made his return.

Despite his remarkable commitment to rebuilding United, Jimmy remained as Wales manager and guided his side through to the quarter-finals of the 1958 World Cup, where they were defeated by Brazil.

Rejecting several lucrative job offers from Italian side Juventus and even the Brazilian national side, Jimmy remained as Welsh manager until 1963.

After a long and loyal service to his beloved United, Jimmy Murphy retired in September 1971.

Even though he had put away his coaching manual, Jimmy was still a part of Manchester United in a scouting role, which he kept until shortly before his death in November 1989.

PRINT AND BE DAMNED.

I have upset a few people during my reporting years with the Leader.

Well it was par for the writing course.

Mind you some people went to any lengths to try and stop their names getting in the newspaper.

Threats, bribes and even trying to get a burglar's name free from the "Look who's Been in Court" pages by saying that his grandmother was dying and the shock would finish her off.

Which of course was never true.

But there were however three little words that would set off a rampant red Rhondda mist on certain valley folk.

They were....

"The Other Valley" or to be proper politically correct "The Rhondda Fach".

If ever we carried a report which said something along the headlines that the "other valley was lacking a railway line or a sports centre" (before the Tylorstown Sports Centre was built) the office phones would start to ring with these sort of calls..

"We are NOT "The Other Valley".We are Rhondda Fach."
"Stop saying "The Other Valley".
"We are not a poor relation".
"We may not be as big as the Fawr but don't call us "The Other Valley."
And on it went.

And so it came to publish pass that "The Other Valley" was decidedly ditched and was forever forgotten.

A SINGLE ON A PONY.

MY years of Rhondda reporting taught me that the valley's lawbreakers could not be labelled as the brightest.

Take this pair that made the Leader pages way back when...

It was around Christmas time 2001 when a blotto bloke decided to head home after a Christmas party.

He couldn't be bothered to catch a bus or a train and a taxi was way off his beaten track.

You would have thought the only way home left was Shank's Pony.

Oh No!

Not this guzzled guy.

Forget Shanks' Pony he went and hitched a ride on a proper pony.

Well a horse anyway.

It was reported that he helped himself to a horse from a field and somehow managed to mount it.

Stunned pedestrians and mortified motorists called the police after the boozed up bloke was seen riding bareback and without a bridle along the valley's main road.

He was seen weaving through the traffic while "hanging on to the horse for dear life."

Police eventually put a stop to the drunken horseplay and he was reined in.

He was brought before valley magistrates charged with being drunk in charge of a horse.and also being drunk and disorderly.

Unbelievable!

And this happened to a brainless burglar back in 2002.

A house was burgled and among a television and other valuables taken was the homeowner's mobile phone.
The owner came up with a ruse to call his mobile and trick whoever answered to give details about himself.
A man answered the call and without much prompting gave his name and address.
The phone's owner said:"Thanks a lot" before cutting him off and contacting the police.
The coppers didn't take long to find him and the mobile along with the other stolen items.
A police officer said afterwards that it was one of the easiest crimes that they had to solve and wished "all criminals were that daft."
I also remember the story headlined "The Starving Burglar" involving a pensioner.
After breaking into his home the burglar forced the old gent to make him breakfast before making his escape.

GORDON "PUT THE BOMP."

GORDON Mills had a blue plaque placed on his former Rhondda home in 2008 and here is a follow up story I did then about it.
"The Rhondda Civic Society will pay tribute to the Rhondda born manager of world renowned singer Tom Jones when they place a plaque on his former home.
The plaque will be sited on the former Trealaw home of Gordon Mills who died in 1986 aged 51.
Mr Mills, who was born in Madras, not only discovered the Treforest born star but was also a prolific songwriter with one of his smash hits being "It's not Unusual" which put Tom Jones on the road to stardom.

Mills had packed in his job with Rhondda Transport to become part of a popular harmonica group called the Frazer Morton Gang.

While performing with them he met Don Paul and Ronnie Wells and together they formed a trio known as "The Viscounts" who had a British hit with a song called "Who put the Bomp".

The former bus conductor with Rhondda Transport eventually quit the group to become an established song writer in London.

His first hit was "I'll Never Get Over You" recorded by Johnny Kidd and the Pirates, reached number four in the British Charts in 1963.

In 1965 Mills started working with Gerry Dorsey, a singer who had been around for a long time without major success, changing his name to Engelbert Humperdinck.

In the following years he also guided a singer called Gilbert O'Sullivan to chart success.

Gordon Mills died of stomach cancer in 1986.

Gordon Mills' former wife Jo said that he loved to talk about his early life in the Rhondda.

Rhodesian born Jo said: "When he was younger Gordon was very friendly with a boy called Gordon Jones.

"He loved to go fishing and bird watching."

Jo, who was a champion high diver as a youngster, was also runner up in a "'Miss South Africa" competition.

At just 17-years-old, Jo came to England in search of a modelling career but found it hard to earn a decent living. She eventually joined the famous Bluebell Dance troupe and moved to Las Vegas to dance at the famous 'Stardust Hotel'

After a few years, Jo returned to London and her modelling career took off.

Jo was at the height of her career when she met Gordon at a party given by singer Terry Dene.

Following their marriage in 1962 she saved up and bought him his first piano and together they wrote songs with singer Lou Reed including "It's Not Unusual".

They remained as man and wife for 21 years before they were divorced.

She said:"He loved talking about the valley and was never happier than when he was back home in the Rhondda."

WHEN ALI BEAT ALAN.

THIS is a story I did in 2011 about the time Rhondda darts player Alan Evans went head to head with World Heavyweight Boxing champion Mohammad Ali

In July 1977, a Rhondda darts player stepped up to the oche in the Gipsy Stadium in the North of England to take on World heavyweight boxing legend Muhammad Ali in an exhibition match.

Rhondda-born Alan Evans was only allowed to score points from hitting trebles in the match which Ali won by hitting the Bullseye.

After winning, the boxing legend immediately proclaimed himself world darts champion.

During the 1970s and 1980s, Alan Evans was a force to be reckoned with on the British darts circuit.

Evans was one of the first players to appear on televised darts, reaching the final of the 1972 News of the World Championship – the first event to be shown in the UK.

He also won the 1975 British Open, which was the first televised event on the BBC. In 1973 and 1974, he reached the final of the darts event on Yorkshire Television's Indoor League.

He won the Winmau World Masters in 1975 – which, along with the News of the World, were the most prestigious titles in darts before the World Championship began in 1978.

When the Darts World Cup began in 1977, the Welsh team of Evans, Leighton Rees and David "Rocky" Jones won the Team Championship and Overall Championship.

Evans was a participant at the inaugural Embassy World Championship.

He defeated Alan Glazier before losing to eventual champion, and close pal Leighton Rees in the quarter-finals.

At the 1979 World Championship, Ynysybwl born Rees again defeated Evans this time in the semi-finals.

In the 1970s Ferndale-born Evans appeared on the Johnny Carson Show in America.

However, his appearance was short lived after he angrily walked off the stage after being asked to throw darts between his legs.

"I'm a darts player not a clown," he told Carson.

Leighton Rees, who died in 2003, once said: "From when I first met Alan at Tonypandy Workingmen's Club in 1970, I knew he was special".

Alan died in April 1999, at the age of 49.

THE SKY HIGH STORIES.

I did my fair share of UFO stories for the Leader.

My editor loved any unexpected tales of unknown flying objects invading the Rhondda skies.

And it always seemed to be me that got the phone call which usually went something like this....

Caller:"Want a great story about a UFO sighting?"

Me:(Sighing)"Fire away".
Caller:"Saw one last night. A huge green thing it was with flashing red lights.Couldn't believe my eyes."
Me:"Where did you see it?"
Caller:"It shot across the sky above Gelli and then I saw it hovering over Penrhys. Really scary it was."
Me:"Tell me what time was this?"
Caller:"Must have been around eleven o'clock last night.
"I had been down the club for a drinking session with the boys and saw it when I was walking home."
Now where have I heard that one before?
Mind you I did get one call from a lady who swore black and blue that she saw a UFO way up in the Stanleytown sky.
The mystery was solved when it turned out to be a Chinese Lantern which I am told are often mistaken for UFOs.
Oh Well!

STRAIGHT TALKING WITH "THE SISTERS."

THE Beverley Sisters were set to perform at the Park and Dare theatre way back when.
I was chosen to go and interview Joy, Teddie and Babs who at the time must have all been in their late sixties.
Before the planned interview I had a call from a hard nosed news editor in Cardiff who said:"When you interview them I don't want a story about all their brilliant show biz stuff.
"Ask them why they are still performing at their age?
"Have they got to perform because they need the money? and "They are past their sing by date so why don't they pack it in and leave it to the youngsters?"
For me the question was:"How am I going to get away with asking that?"
It might be a very short interview.

My mother loved the Beverley Sisters. What would she have thought?

I enjoyed the show and after the last strains of "Sisters" died away their agent agreed for the interview to be done and I went back stage to meet the trio.

I was warmly greeted by a big smiling Joy who said:"Right darling. What do you want to know?"

Here goes...

Did I get away with asking those questions?

Just about.

ROCK ON KEN.

I could never write a book without making a mention of Rhondda's one and only Ken "Rock n' Roll" Williams

Myself and Ken, go back a long Bill Haley way.

Back in the 1960s we delivered Sunday newspapers and comics from a pair of pulverised prams around Ystrad for Hackers newsagents in Ton Pentre.

We were delivering Tiger comics when Roy of the Rovers was playing in the Melchester Rovers youth side.

Down through the Leader years I penned a few stories about Ken and I enjoyed everyone of them.

Keep on rockin' Ken.

CHAPTER 8
ME AND "THE PADDINGTON EXPRESS."

DURING my reporting life I would getting invited to the Welsh Ex Boxers Association re-union which was held in the Rhydyfelin Labour Club and more recently at the Taffs Well Ex Servicemen's club.

They were always knockout occasions with boxing greats including Dai Dower, Howard Winston and Robbie Regan getting in the rounds.

I was there some fighting years back on the lookout for former boxers who could give an interesting interview.

It was then I spotted Terry Downes.

London born Downes was known as the "Paddington Express" for his aggressive fighting style and held the world middleweight title for ten months from 1961 to 1962.

He starred in several films usually playing a thug, villain or bodyguard.

And so I went over to Terry's table where he was sat with some of his boxing pals.

"Excuse me Mr Downes," I asked," I am a reporter with the local newspaper and I wonder if I......."

That was as far as it got.

Terry pushed his chair back, stood up raised his fists and snarled:"Outside now.Come on just you and me."

Now he was around ten years older than me but I knew it would be a no contest.

Surely he wouldn't hit a reporter with glasses on.

Thankfully a "Good Boxing Samaritan" stepped in between us and pulled me to one side.

"Sorry about that," he said,"Terry doesn't mean it. It just happens now and again".

I couldn't get to the bar quickly enough to gulp down a shandy on the rocks.

MISSING BADGE OF HONOUR.

"BAA-BAAS TRY HERO LOST OUT ON HIS BADGE BECAUSE HE HAD TO GET HIS BUS HOME

That was the headline I did for a Leader story back in 2013. Here it is...

"A schoolteacher who scored a try for the Barbarians in their win over the mighty All Blacks in 1973 has told how he failed to get his "badge of honour" because he had to pay for the bus fare home.

Tylorstown-born John Bevan, who is a teacher at Monmouth school, was a member of the Barbarians team which beat New Zealand 23-11 in a match played at Cardiff Arms Park.

John, who attended Ferndale Grammar School as a youngster, scored a try while playing in the wing position during that famous victory in 1973.

His memories were stirred following an interview with Pontypridd veteran Tommy David, who played a key role in scoring that celebrated try.

John recalled: "That was a very special time in my rugby career.

"It was special to score a try and also be part of a team which beat the All Blacks."

After picking up his first rugby ball with Tylorstown, he went on to play for the Cardiff College of Education side and also the Cardiff team.

After being capped for Wales in 1971 he toured Australia and New Zealand with the British Lions.

He played in 14 matches including the first test and scored a total of 18 tries.

During his international career Bevan scored five tries for Wales.

In September 1973, Bevan switched to rugby league and joined Warrington for the then massive signing-on fee of £12,000.

He played for Wales and Great Britain.

In September 2000, after having stepped down as director of coaching for the Welsh Rugby Union, John Bevan joined the teaching staff at Monmouth School.

The 63-year-old teacher, who is the brother of RCT councillor Robert Bevan, coaches young rugby players at his school.

He said: "It is hard to believe that it is 40 years ago that I played in the match."

He did recall that after the match he needed to catch a bus to get home to Tylorstown.

Before catching the bus he went to see Barbarians secretary Geoffrey Windsor Lewis.

John said: "I wanted to buy a tie, a gilt button and a blazer badge but after deducting money for the bus fare home I only had enough cash to buy a tie and a gilt button.

"I never did get the badge."

Robert Bevan remembers his dad taking him to the match 40 years ago.

"I was at the match with my dad Gilbert and also the father of rugby legend Gareth Edwards..

"When John scored the try they told me to behave because I became so excited".

TRAPPED MINERS NINE DAY RESCUE.

IN October 2010 the rescue of 33 Chilean miners was met with a blaze of world publicity which prompted me to recall the events in a Rhondda colliery many years ago when five miners were trapped underground for nine days before being rescued.

On the morning of April 11, 1877, water burst through into the workings at Tynewydd pit in Porth.

Of the 14 men underground at that time, two men, John Hughes, 50, and his 18-year-old son William Hughes, along with a number of horses, were drowned in the initial torrent of water.

Faint sounds of tapping could be heard travelling through the coal barrier, confirming that men were still alive on the other side.

This amazing news quickly spread, with the aid of telegraphy, and soon newspaper reporters were descending on the small community to follow the dramatic story.

The rescuers were within hailing distance of the imprisoned men, and were able to confirm that four men and a young boy were trapped – huddled together on a ledge, in a very small cavity on the other side.

The four were David Jenkins, Moses Powell, George and John Thomas, and the boy was David Hughes.

Mr Jenkins, the eldest of the small group and an active member of the local Independent Congregational Chapel, continually reassured led them in the singing of hymns to lift their spirits.

Hunger had forced them to eat the grease from their candles, but now even that meagre sustenance was long gone, and they were on the point of complete exhaustion.

The rescue team decided to drill holes through the barrier to gauge the distance left to tunnel, and also to facilitate a tube so that liquid food could be passed through to the desperately hungry trapped miners

The flames in their Clanny lamps flared dangerously with the amount of gas present.

Fearing the possibility of an immediate explosion, the rescuers were ordered to retreat.

It wasn't until the following day that conditions improved enough to allow the rescue attempt to resume.

The leader of the four men on shift, Isaac Pride, took it upon himself to be the man to break down the remaining barrier. This dangerous operation had to be performed in complete darkness because of the fear of escaping gas.

Abraham "Abby" Dodd and Gwilym Thomas assisted him by carrying the safety lamps showing light as far as the coal face, a distance of 40 yards, and then were told to retreat behind the sets of air doors, leaving Mr Pride to carry out his task in darkness.

When Mr Pride's pick broke through the barrier, the initial blast of escaping air threw him back against the air door. He quickly recovered and set about enlarging the hole.

By this time, Mr Dodd had come to assist, and they climbed through the hole to where they found the trapped five miners who were too weak to even stand.

Between them and the escape hole, which had been made above by Mr Pride, was a narrow deep channel filled with floodwater.

With no time to lose, because the flood water had now began to rise again, Mr Pride stretched his body across this gap, forming a human bridge that allowed Mr Dodd to pull the five across to safety.

They had been trapped for over nine days.

Every man involved was a hero, and for the particular outstanding part in the rescue played by Isaac Pride, John Howell and Daniel Thomas, each were given the Albert Medal of the 1st class, and 21 of the other rescuers the Albert Medal, 2nd class.

This was the first time the Albert Medal had been awarded for gallantry underground.

Isaac Pride was killed in an accident at Cymmer Colliery in the late 1890s.

Daniel Thomas was killed in an explosion, along with 13 others at the Naval Colliery, Penygraig, in 1884.

Quite a story.

SUPERMAN'S DAD IN PORTH.

DID you know Superman's "earth" grandmother was from Pontypridd?

Film star Glenn Ford, who played Superman's "earth" father Jonathan Kent in the epic movie "Superman", was born Gwyllyn Samuel Newton Ford in Quebec to his Pontypridd born mother named Hannah.

The budding movie star was eventually asked to change his name by a Hollywood director because Gwyllyn was too difficult to pronounce.

It was the name Glenn Ford which became big among the acting credits on the silver screen during the 1950s and 1960s with films including "Blackboard Jungle", "The Big Heat" and my favourite "The 3.10 to Yuma" which I saw sat in the ninepennies in the pictures at Nantymoel Workmen's Hall in 1957.

Glenn who died in 2006 aged 90 will also be remembered for playing Clark Kent's father in the 1978 "Superman" movie.

And I can also remember doing a story about the Hollywood star visiting the Rhondda many years ago when he sat on a bench in Porth to do a documentary about the valley.

I interviewed someone living in the street where Glenn was doing the documentary who told me he "couldn't believe his eyes at first".

He said: "It is not every day you see a Hollywood superstar walking along a Porth street."

ALBY IS A LEGEND.

YOU cannot talk about the history of Rhondda Boys' Clubs without mentioning the name Alby Nicholas.

"Alby Nick" as he was more familiarly known was a stalwart and much more of Treorchy Boys' Club and also synonymous with boys' clubs throughout the valley.

Here is what Pentre born and former Wales and Swansea soccer player Alan Curtis said about Alby in a project called "A History of the Boys' Clubs Movement in Wales."

"I owe a lot of my success to the grounding I had at Treorchy Boys' Club.

"I spent six happy years at the club and loved every bit of it. It wasn't just the football, which was obviously important, but all the great friends I made there who are still great friends to this day.

"It was at the Boys' Club where I came into contact with the late great Alby Nicholas who worked tirelessly for decades for the sheer love of it".

Alby was awarded the BEM for his services to the club and I remember his devotion to Treorchy Boys' Club with great affection"

Whenever I am in the company of Treorchy born World Cup referee Clive Thomas he always talks about the influence Alby had on him and how much he respected him.

I only met Alby a couple of times but I could sense that he was a remarkable man who showed great devotion to the Boys' Clubs movement in the valley.

"GOT PEN AND PAPER HANDY?"

MY working life as a reporter was never dull.
Many times this happened...
Telephone caller:"Can I speak to a reporter?"
Me:"You are speaking to one."
Caller:"Do you wanna good story?"
"Yep"
"Got pen and paper handy?"
There was something wrong if I hadn't.
I never knew who I was going to meet in reception.
And of course I would stop people in their talking tracks when they would say:"Don't put this in the Leader but did you know..?"
Hold it! If I don't know about I can't do a story on it.

THE ITALIAN CONNECTION.

THERE was always fun and games when the Bonny Babies competition came around.

It was on the Tarot Cards that there would be a mix up with names or ages

And of course there was always that heart stopping moment when the paper had just "been put to bed" when you had a dreadful feeling you may have reported a name wrong or some other costly mistake.

I always maintained that I could walk into any pub or club in the Rhondda and come out with a fistful of brilliant stories.

Still I wouldn't have changed my reporting life for the world.

I loved writing about Rhondda's "Italian Connection."

Growing up in Nantymoel I spent most of my young life sipping a Vimto and eating a steamed pie in a "Bracchis".

So whenever Wales played Italy in rugby, soccer or any other sport it was down to me to contact the valley's Bracchis to find out which team their allegiance was with.

To me the Bracchis are as much a part of valley communities as the collieries, the choirs and even the sheep which used to roam the streets knocking over dust bin lids.

I first heard of President Kennedy's assassination in 1963 on a crackling wireless set in a Nantymoel Bracchis.

I made many Italian friends during my reporting years among them was Aldo Bacchetta who with his brother Ron owned a popular restaurant in Porth.

In the 1950s Aldo served, with twin brother Mario, in Berlin with the Royal Welsh Fusiliers.

Returning to Wales, he continued in the family business and became involved in many activities outside the shop.

He joined Players Anonymous and his interest in valley life led him to co-publish books on Old Rhondda.

Aldo, who sadly died in 2009, bestowed a special honour on me by giving me a much sought after "Rhondda Visitor's PastPorth" which "permitted and warmly invited me to visit all parts of the Rhondda."

Even better than being given the "Freedom of the Borough."

I miss my steamed pies in the Bracchis but much more than that I miss Aldo.

In 2008 I reported that an Italian-owned cafe which has been trading in Treorchy for almost 90 years was about to serve its last Cappuccino.

The Cosy Cafe in High Street owned by Luigi and Marilyn Balestrazzi was a Bracchis which was set to disappear from the Rhondda landscape.

The cafe was first opened in 1919 by brothers Dom and Joe Balestrazzi and was called the Balestrazzi Brothers.

Joe eventually opened up the Station Cafe in Treorchy, which is still trading and owned by his son Dom.

Luigi started work in his father Dom's cafe after leaving school, where he was helped by his late brother John.

Luigi said at the time: "Down through the years the customers who have regularly visited the shop have become friends.

"Marilyn and I are sad to leave but feel the time is right to retire.

"We have spent wonderful times behind the counter in the cafe and we are very grateful to all the customers who have supported us down through the years.

"We are one of many Italian families which have bonded in the South Wales Valleys and it has been a privilege to have been part of that.

"There have been many changes over the years. I can remember the time when Treorchy used to be buzzing with activity late on a Sunday night."

TO BIRO OR NOT TO BIRO?

I suppose I am one of many which think that today's political correctness is bonkers.

But many Maerdy moons ago I fell foul of a something similar to political correctness.

During my reporting years with the Leader there were some words linked to brands which were strictly taboo.

For instance you could never report that somebody had used "a Stanley Knife" instead it had to be "a craft knife".

You could not use "Portakabin" it had to be "portable cabin".

I was once even taken to task by a news editor because I used a ladies darts team in my report.

I was told to change it to a women's darts team because the word "ladies" was only for "females who had a title".

It came to the crunch one time when I used the word Biro in my weekly column.

A couple of weeks after the column was published my editor received a letter from a London based solicitor warning me not to use the word Biro again or legal action would be taken.

In future I had to write "ball point pen".

If someone in Mayfair was reading my column they must have been really sad.

Sorry but a ball point pen will always be a Biro to me.

The biggest lie in the world at one time was:"There's a cheque in the post" but nowadays it is:"The computers are down."

To my way of thinking:"You can't beat the biro."

"NO PIC-HE'S ON THE SICK."

AS well as news I also had to look after the sports coverage with the Leader.

Most Saturdays myself and a photographer would be at a valley rugby match come rain or shine.

It always seemed more often rain than shine.

This happened after one particular match.

The Monday morning following the match I had finished my report and the pictures were all set for the sports page when I got a frantic phone call from a club secretary.

He said:" Dave are you going to put photos of Saturday's game in the Leader?"

"Errr....Yes."

"Are you going to use a photo of our scrum half?"

"Yes I am.It's a cracking action shot of him diving with the rugby ball behind a scrum."

"You can't "shreiked he.

"What do you mean I can't?"

"Our scrum half is on the sick and if that photo is shown to his doctor he will sign him off."

Oh No!

Hold the sports page!!

SHOE TIME IN THE VALLEY

IN 2010 I interviewed a Ferndale senior citizen about the precious memories he had of working in a Rhondda footwear factory which once employed hundreds of workers. Graham Matthews started work in the Treforest Fashion Novelty factory in Dinas when he left school at the age of 15.

The factory made women's and children's shoes as well as handbags.

The factory then changed its name to Trefano and moved from Dinas to Williamstown.

Mr Matthews said: "It was a thriving factory with the workers, who were all local, like one big happy family."

Mr Matthews said that he met his wife Glenys, 74, who also worked at the factory for several years.

He recalled that when he returned to the factory after a "Miners Holiday" in 1980 he was told that the factory, which had then become Clarks Footwear, was closing.

He said: "It was a sad time with between 200 and 300 workers losing their jobs."

"I worked there for 30 happy years so I suppose I do know a lot about ladies footwear.

"The styles have changed quite a lot over the years."

BERNARD AND A PACK OF LAGER.

IN the late nineties a film company called Bangaw wanted to make a TV series called "Into the Valley" for BBC Wales.

As part of the series they wanted to do show a day in the life of a local newspaper reporter.

I didn't even have to audition before I got the part.

I was filmed going to different parts of the valley to interview people and much to my embarrassment I got lost trying to track down a person I needed to talk to.

Another part of the series focussed on the trials and tribulations at the Trealaw Workingmen's Club better known as the "Rez".

I had a meeting with the club committee to find a way to raise much needed funds.

It was decided to hold a special fundraising event and they were fortunate enough to get well known comedian Bernard Manning to take part.

I was told that following the event Bernard couldn't start his car because of a flat battery and needed some of the club members to give him a push to get it started.

It reminded me of my Swansea Gazette years when a club manager contacted me to say Bernard was appearing there and would I like to do an interview.

Bernard was due on stage at 10pm so myself and a photographer arrived outside the club at about 9.30pm where we were met by the manager.

Anyway 9.45 came and went and there was still no sign of Bernard.

With the clock clicking down quicker than the manager's fingernails a car pulled up a few minutes before 10pm and out stepped the heavyweight comedian.

"Who are you?" he asked glaring at me.

"I'm a newspaper reporter and this is the photographer?"

"And you?" he asked pointing to the manager.

"I'm the manager."

Pointing at me he said:"You and the snapper follow me."

Pointing at the manager he said:"You can get me a pack of lager."

I interviewed Bernard in his vest and underpants while he was changing to go on stage.

It was not a sight for sore eyes.

As soon as the interview was over Bernard walked on stage with lager in hand in front of a packed hall.

What a performer.

SYBIL BURTON'S VALLEY ROOTS

IN 2003 I did a story about the Rhondda born first wife of actor Richard Burton who died at the age of 83.

Sybil Christopher, born Williams, was an erstwhile actress and in later life became a theatre producer.

But she was thrust into the public eye when her then husband began a whirlwind romance with Elizabeth Taylor, prompting a dramatic, painful and expensive divorce.

Born in Tylorstown on March 27, 1929, the miner's daughter met her first husband on the set of his first film, The Last Days of Dolwyn, in 1948.

Sybil, then a student at the London Academy of Music and Dramatic Art, was cast as an extra while Burton was still a relative unknown.

She married Burton at just 19 and the couple moved to Fulham together. While Sybil continued acting for a time, with roles including voicing Myfanwy Price in a radio version of Under Milk Wood in 1954, she eventually gave up her stage career, preferring to move with Burton to America as a wife.

Remembering her decision, she told the New York Times in 1994: "It was very clear to me that I wasn't making a sacrifice. I knew that Richard would have an exciting career and that it would be fun, two Welsh kids on the Queen Mary, travelling first class."

But in 1963, as a result of Burton's relationship with Taylor, Sybil successfully sued for divorce on the grounds of abandonment and cruel and inhuman treatment, winning custody of their two daughters and a settlement of $1m.

After the divorce, she relocated to New York where she became something of an entrepreneur in the world of theatre and disco, setting up the New Theatre and nightclub Arthur in New York in the 1960s.

In 1964 she married actor and singer Jordan Christopher, with whom she had a third child.

In 1991, she founded the Bay Street Theatre in Sag Harbor, New York.

There, she served as artistic director for 22 years. In a statement on the theatre's website, she was described as "the heart and soul" of the theatre.

It added: "[She] will not only be missed by all her friends at Bay Street Theatre but also by the entire Sag Harbor Village community. Our thoughts are with her family that she loved dearly."

CHAPTER 9
POETS AT HEART

WE used to receive lots of poems at the Leader office and we always did our best to try and publish them.

I always thought that everyone in the Rhondda was a poet at heart.

Whatever happened in the world someone from the Rhondda would write a poem about it.

One in particular I received was from a woman who penned a glowing poem about the Rhondda Valley.

At the end of the poem she wrote:"I got my inspiration for this poem from that wonderful book and film "How Green Was My FAMILY."

Oops!

Another rhyme time was a poem that began with the line:"I came to the Rhondda so lovely and green.

To make a better life for me and Irene."

And I can't forget the music lovers.

Like the chap who send me a CD of his song renditions.

The stand out one was his version of the Tom Jones' hit "The Green, Green, Grass of Home"

Which went:"The old home town looks the same,

As I stepped down from the PLANE",

Couldn't have been Ponty.

Oh Well!

DES'S MARDY PIT MEMORIES.

ALWAYS a pleasure to meet Des Dutfield whenever I am pounding the streets of Ponty.

This is a story I did on Des back in December 2010.

"Twenty years after the closure of Mardy Colliery, a former president of the National Union of Miners has shared his vivid memories.

Des Dutfield, of Trebanog Road, Trebanog, said: "It was the last pit in the Rhondda to close and that prompted a media frenzy."

British Coal shut Mardy down on December 21, 1990, resulting in 600 miners losing their jobs.

The Mardy colliers had the reputation of being the most militant in Britain, earning Maerdy its nickname of "Little Moscow".

When the colliery closed that Christmas week, a brass band played The Internationale, a famous socialist, communist, anthem and the people vowed they would not be beaten down.

Mr Dutfield said: "The union, the miners and their families fought to the bitter end to save the Mardy pit but it was a losing battle.

"The Government tried every way they could to prevent a confrontation.

"They tried to tempt the miners with redundancy packages among other offers this but they would not give in.

"I have always considered the Mardy colliery to be synonymous with the Rhondda mining industry.

"Maerdy has always been a very proud and close-knit community and that spirit shone through in the battle to save the pit."

A miner for 35 years, Mr Dutfield followed his father and his grandfathers into the pit.

He was a coal face worker at the Lewis Merthyr Colliery until its closure in 1983, and was later transferred to Abercynon. He was elected vice-president and finally president of the South Wales Union of Mineworkers.

The last coal was raised at Mardy Colliery in 1986 although coal continued to be mined and brought to the surface at Tower Drift Mine in Hirwaun.

Mr Dutfield said: "I suppose there are many children living in the Rhondda who have never seen a coal fire, but they should never be deprived of knowing about its proud mining heritage.

"When the pit closed there were hopes that other industries would be tempted to set up in the top end of the Rhondda Fach".

"The battle to save Mardy Colliery is something that should never be forgotten."

A PRECIOUS GATEWAY.

HERE'S one of my stories I did in 2008 about the Rhondda Gateway Club which does wonderful work in the valley.

Dorothy Williams, who worked for the Social Services decided to form a Gateway Club in 1972 to support people with learning difficulties.

Despite her hard work the club wasn't successful and she was forced to admit defeat.

Two years later a regional officer of the National Society of Mencap gave an inspired talk at a parents meeting which encouraged Mrs Williams to try again.

The first meeting was held in the vestry of Salem Chapel, Llwynypia where 15 members and six helpers were present. Mencap donated an initial loan of £100 and the Gateway Club was officially launched.

Sadly Mrs Williams didn't live long enough to witness the success the club has achieved over the past 35 years.

In 1975, Bryn John and his wife Jean become involved with the club after bringing a group of young people from a local chapel to entertain the members.

Bryn, who had a strong musical background, quickly realised that the members loved their music.

The club committee asked Bryn if he would form a musical group within the club.

Under Bryn's direction the club members formed an impressive musical group playing instruments including, tambourines, maracas and a washboard.

Bryn also discovered that among the 20 members there were several with good singing voices.

After two years of rehearsing the group gave their first public performance in 1977 at the senior citizens hall in Llwynypia.

Seasoned valley performers Dennis Stallard and Cheryl Wigley gave their support to the group and over the following years the members performed in more than 400 concerts in the South Wales area.

The group also represented Wales at the Festival Hall in London on three occasions and also performed at the Edinburgh Festival.

In 1975 Mal Turner became club leader and he introduced sporting activities into the club.

Under Mal's leadership members enjoyed great success in sports events and he was also one of the organisers of music and drama festivals held annually at Porthcawl.

Another club stalwart was the late Mal Rees who was the club's president for many years and who was hugely respected by everyone.

Another good friend of the Gateway club was the late Brian Morris who was popularly known as the Easter Egg man

who worked tirelessly for 46 years during which he distributed 120,000 Easter Eggs for disabled people.
Following the sad loss of Mal Rees Joyce Brewer took over as president and Bryn John could not praise enough the effort she has done to make the club a success.
Joyce, who has been also club leader and treasurer for the past 18 years works tirelessly arranging trips for club members and also raising much needed funds.

A CUPPA FROM YVETTE.

WHILE at the Rhondda Leader news desk I received a call from RAID (Rhondda Against Illegal Drugs) asking if I knew of any way their newly opened cafe in Pentre could get more publicity.

Not long after I put the phone down I spotted an advert about a panto in Swansea which starred Vicki Michelle.
I thought it would be a great idea if I could get Vicki, who played waitress Yvette in the TV series "Allo Allo" to pay a visit to the café. With that in mind I contacted her agent and asked if that was possible.

He told me that Vicki was very busy with rehearsals but he would ask her.

The following day he got back to me and I was delighted to be told that Vicki would like to take up the offer.

And so it came to pass that the Cafe Rene waitress became the Cafe Raid waitress for an unforgettable few hours.

There was quite a crowd in the cafe and Vicki was fantastic. She served the tea and coffee and chatted to everyone.

Everyone admired the fact that despite being on a very tight schedule performing in the panto she still found time to make a visit to a Rhondda cafe.

It was a lovely story.

MEETING UP WITH MINTER.

WHEN I was invited to the annual Welsh Ex Boxers Association Event a couple of years ago I managed to have an interview with former World Middleweight Champion Alan Minter.

After Terry Downes had threatened to "knock my block off" a little earlier it was nice to be able to chat to Alan.

On 16 March 1980, in Las Vegas, Minter was given a shot at World Middleweight Champion Vito Antuofermo's title at the Caesars Palace.

 He won the title by a 15-round decision and, in a rematch, he retained the world title by a TKO (Technical Knock Out) in eight rounds.

Minter's run as world champion ended when he was stopped in three rounds by Marvin Hagler at Wembley Arena in London.

COPYING BRIAN BLESSED.

THE brood badgered me to adopt a dog a few years ago and I got some help from a "lead" story I had written in 2010.

And so I was collared to go visiting some dog refuges and despite perusing some pitiful pooches the Edwards' home was still dogless.

It was then that I spotted an advert about a dog show being held in Gilfach Goch by the Friends of the Animals RCT group.

Friends of the Animals is a small independent rescue group and was started by Eileen Jones when her tagged, microchipped and unspayed Yorkshire Terrier, Sophie, disappeared without trace in 2003.

Which reminded me of a story I did about, renowned thunder voiced actor Brian Blessed adopting a "wonky dog" from the Rhondda based group.

The actor and animal lover heard about an elderly poodle called Titch being housed in Wonky Towers by the group and decided to give him a home.

Friends of the Animals founder member Eileen Jones said: "When we adopted Titch into our Wonky Dog club section we were worried because he was quite elderly and needed a lot of dental treatment.

"Titch wasn't with us very long before we had a call to say that Brian Blessed would like to have Titch.

" He had heard about Titch's plight from his agent and decided to give him a home at his place in Berkshire".

And so it came to pass that we did go to the dog show and doggone it we did end up with a furry family member.

His name is Alfie and he is a half and half hound. He is part Irish Wolfhound (or Deerhound according to my old Ponty mate and former copper David Hicks) and Lurcher.

It was initially decided that we would get a lap dog.

Some lap dog!!

The Edwards clan have nothing but admiration for the Friends of the Animals group who do some truly amazing efforts to re-home animals.

MEL AND FOOTBALL CARDS.

FOOTBALL cards-remember them?

Back in the 1950s I used to have a prized collection which included Stanley Matthews, Billy Wright and Nat Lofthouse among others.

But I never did get one of a Rhondda football legend who died in 2010.

Ystrad born Mel Hopkins was a Rhondda Boys Clubs player before he was snapped up by Tottenham Hotspur in 1951 as a £3 a week apprentice.

He was with the London club for nearly 14 years and played with and against some of the greatest names of that era.

These included Stanley Matthews, Tom Finney, Jimmy Greaves, Bobby Charlton and George Best.

Mel played for Wales between 1956 and 1963, earning 34 caps, and featured at the 1958 World Cup in Sweden, where they lost narrowly to Brazil, including a young Pele, in the quarter-finals.

The valley born player sustained a serious facial injury when went up for an aerial challenge with Scotland centre forward Ian St John at Hampden Park in November 1959.

St John's forehead made high-velocity contact with Hopkins' face, shattering his nose and breaking his jaw.

The injury forced him out of immediate first-team contention and allowed his English rival Ron Henry to usurp his club place in the long term.

Thus the Welshman was confined to the sidelines in 1960-61 as Spurs became the first side in modern times to win the coveted League and FA Cup double.

Although living in Worthing Mel, who died in 2010 aged 75, often visited his mother in Ystrad.

I had the pleasure of having a chat with him when we bumped into each other in a model railway show in Ystrad Sports Centre on one of his last trips to the Rhondda.

Mel is much missed.

THE RAILROAD RUNS...

DO you remember an Alma Cogan song called :"The Railroad runs through the Middle of the House?"
It was quite popular in the 1950s.
Well I once tracked a story about a model railroad running through the middle of a Treorchy house.
It proved to be a "train of thought" for me.
The Treorchy house in question belonged to retired architect and model railway buff Bernard Davies.
Bernard had this amazing model railway layout in which a model train travelled from room to room in his lovely home.
It even came to halt at a station in the toilet.
The station of course was named WaterLOO.
Bernard, who always put a lot of hard work into organising the South Wales Model show whenever it came to the Rhondda, had a great passion for his chosen hobby.
Haydn Shadbolt was also another "model citizen" I had the pleasure to meet.
Haydn, who lived in Trealaw with his lovely wife Glenys, was not only a great supporter of model railways but also worked tirelessly as a member of the Friends of the Rhondda Heritage Park.
Haydn also made sure I was looked after whenever I joined the Boot Sales which were held on Sunday mornings at the Rhondda Heritage Park.
They were a lovely couple.
As for me?
Well I can remember not only steam trains but also clockwork trains particularly when it was Christmas Day morning at my home in Nantymoel..

When I was in short trousers I had, I think it was a Hornby clockwork train set for Christmas, along with a Blow Football game and a Hopalong Cassidy watch.
See how spoilt I was

PAUL IS AN INSPIRATION.

DURING my years with the Leader I became good friends with Paul Knight.
Former Wales and Pontypridd rugby player Paul, has battled Multiple Sclerosis for more than twenty years.
Having worn Aberavon colours before moving to Ponty, Trealaw born Paul played five times for Wales and also for the Barbarians before joining Treorchy, where his playing career was ended when he was told that he was in the initial stages of Multiple Sclerosis.
No longer was Paul faced with the challenges on a rugby field but facing a much bigger opponent in the form of MS.
Paul recently reminded me of a certain afternoon way back in 2008 when we first met and we were both on the carpet.
It was on one of my final reporting trips up the Rhondda before retiring when I decided to give him a shout.
I arrived at his home in Rhys Street, Trealaw and knocked on the door.
Silence.
Knocked again.
Then Paul's voice came booming through passage.
"Come in the door is open."
When I entered the room Paul was sat on the carpet with his daughter Nadia struggling to get him sat back up on a settee.
"Hiya Dai," he greeted me as I knelt down to shake hands with him.

Paul had somehow slipped off the settee and was unable to get up from the floor.

Despite Nadia and I struggling to get Paul back on the settee we were unable to do it.

Nadia then rang Paul's wife Jennifer, who was working in Tonypandy Library, to come to the rescue and eventually we three got Paul back on the settee.

From that carpet day forth Paul and I have become firm friends.

A few years ago I had a chance meeting with former Wales, Leeds and Swansea footballer Alan Curtis and when I mentioned Paul he wanted to pay him a visit.

Even after I put a full stop to my final Leader story Paul and I have remained firm friends and I always look forward to visiting him in his specially adapted home in Ystrad.

When Paul was a patient at Rookwood hospital I along with Wales and Ponty rugby legend Tom David paid him a visit. After the visit Tom described Paul as "an inspiration."

THERE'S ONLY ONE JOHNNY BENNETT.

I lived a few doors away from well known valley singer Johnny Bennett in Trealaw and I spent many a happy hour chatting to him not only doing interviews for the Leader but also on social occasions.

Johnny had a legion of stories about his connections with Tom Jones, Engelbert Humperdinck and Gordon Mills among others.

The last time I met Johnny was in the NUM club when somebody called him Tony Bennett.

"No I'm Johnny," he said, "Tony has got more money than me".

Many will fondly remember Johnny singing not only in valley clubs but also further afield.

He was always great company and I always had the best of welcome from him and his lovely wife Sonia.

I always talk about the remarkable people I met during my years with the Leader and Johnny Bennett is one of them.

IVOR AND THAT SPANISH SWIM.

WHEN my young daughter Fay took some swimming lessons at the Rhondda Sports Centre back in the 1980s she was coached by Ivor Sutton.

Although Fay was very nervous when she went into the water Ivor re-assured her every watery step of the way.

He was an absolute marvel not only with Fay but all the youngsters he took under his water wings.

And so rummaging through the Rhondda Leader archives recently I came across this story about Ivor.

Here it is....

"Rhondda's one-legged, long-distance swimmer, Ivor Sutton, aged 36, turned into bed at breakfast time today tired "but very happy" after a long distance river swim in Spain.

He was invited to take part in the swim by the Spanish Swimming Association.

He came 12th out of 26 competitors, and was presented with a large cup and trophy.

The swim was part of Ivor's build-up for next month's attempt to swim the English Channel.

The Rhondda swimmer was accompanied home to Tylorstown from Cardiff after his weekend visit to Spain by soccer referee Clive Thomas, who travelled on the same London to Cardiff train as the swimmer.

Ivor, a factory worker, married with two children, lost his leg when he was seven years of age."

Ivor Sutton is one of those people you don't forget.

He made his own special mark on the Rhondda.

It was a privilege to know him.

RAINING ON NOBBY'S PARADE.

I took up an invite to attend a special evening held by Blaenrhondda Football Club at the Tynewydd Labour Club.

I was looking forward to it because the special guest was former England and World Cup Football winner Nobby Stiles.

I arrived early for the event and sat down with some club members anticpating the night ahead.

Shortly afterwards a door opened and a short bespectacled man poked his head into the room.

"Hello," said one of the members,"Can I help at all?"

After I realised who the stranger was I nudged him and whispered:"That's Nobby Stiles."

When the truth finally dawned Nobby was given a warm welcome.

Eventually when all the top table guests had arrived we were told to stand tight until we were introduced to the audience sat in the main hall.

While the MC was making a speech before the introductions were made me, Nobby and the other guests were herded into a small yard before entering the main hall.

While we were standing there in the open air the heavens opened and down came the Tynewydd rain.

While we waited Nobby looked at his rain splattered suit then looked at me and said:"I don't believe this is happening."

I sat next to Nobby during our meal and he was brilliant company.
He had so many great stories to tell and always made time to talk to the many people who came and shook hands with him.
The England football team were playing that night but he was not interested he wanted to talk about Roy Paul and other Welsh footballers he admired.

ONLY MEN ALLOWED.

GROWING up in Nantymoel I can recall that the Labour Clubs, Con Clubs and Workingmens Clubs were very much men only domains.
But drinking times have changed-or have they?
I did this story back in 2010.
"Members of a Pontypridd club have decided to stick with their men-only policy following a three-day ballot.
The Celtic Club in Mill Street, Pontypridd, will remain "only men allowed" after members decided against allowing women in.
By doing so, they sacrificed funding from the Pontypridd regeneration scheme.
The Rhondda Cynon Taff council scheme includes an enhancement programme which provides opportunities for commercial property owners in the town, including the Celtic Club, to take advantage of financial support of up to 70% towards physically enhancing properties.
Club secretary Paul Davies said: "The voting outcome on remaining a men-only club was quite close, but the decision to accept funding to give the shop units a makeover was overwhelming.

"To renovate the six units we would have to find around £25,000 with the regeneration scheme funding the remainder.

"Although there was funding available to give the club a facelift providing women were allowed in, I think there was a general feeling that renovations included in the regeneration scheme were not really adequate and would not have been a great benefit."

CHAPTER 10
:   A WONDERFUL REPORTING LIFE.

I have enjoyed a "wonderful reporting life."

It gave me the chance to meet some remarkable people and also share in both sad and happy times.

My ride on the reporting rollercoaster saw me threatened and bribed by people desperate to put a full stop to getting their stories published.

But on the other writing hand there were times when I would get a call from someone who would say:"Thanks for doing that story Dave.It has helped a lot."

And those calls were very special.

I always used to say that I could walk into a valley pub or club and come out with a fistful of stories.

I have put my by line to sob stories, human interest stories and heart rending stories while I also got a lot of fun doing my weekly "One Man's Rhondda" column in which I tried to capture on a part of every day life in the valley.

People would often ask me:"Why don't they print happy stories on the front page?" to which I would reply:"Sadly people would rather read shock horror stories."

And of course there were always "too many adverts in the paper" .

Like everything else the passing years saw changes in the reporting game.

In my later reporter years I rarely left the office.

Most of my interviews were done over the telephone.

I was never happy with these "cold interviews" I much preferred sitting on a front room couch doing a face to face interview.

I have to admit that I often shake my head in disbelief when I pick up a morning national newspaper and see a full page spread about a television programme.

But that's the way it is.

THE PORTH GAZETTE.

IT always used to amaze me that people used to ring the office and ask for the "Porth Gazette" which went out of circulation way back when.

And of course for many the name of the paper was "The Rhondda Liar."

Back in the 1980s every Wednesday afternoon I would jump in my Skoda and drive up to Dowlais to "see the paper off".

In those days the compositors or typesetters would paste the pages of the newspaper together on boards and believe me they were a force to be reckoned with.

The "comps" were members of the SOGAT union and I was warned to be very careful while I waited for the pages to be completed.

I think it was on the second occasion that I was overseeing the pages when I noticed a piece of paper had fallen off one of the comps pasteboard.

I was quite near so I picked up the paper and put it back in its place.

As soon as I did a comp walked over to me and said:"If you do that again we will all walk out on strike.

"Now go away and wait until you are called for."

And of course sometimes mistakes happened which I knew should never have happened.

For instance a comp was putting the finishing touches to a front page story about a rather stormy council meeting while the picture on the page was of a woman feeding a donkey.

Before I had chance to thoroughly check the story the page was whipped away and ready for the Press.
When I looked over the paper in the office the following morning I was horrified to read the front page lead story..
Midway through the story it reported that an angry councillor had said:"Hee Haw! Hee Haw!"
I could then see that part of the caption underneath the picture of the woman feeding the donkey was missing.
It didn't take me long to realise how that had happened.
That part of the caption had somehow been included in the front page story.
Was it deliberate?
I will never know.
Then there was another time when a Mayoress was pictured pinning a rosette on a winning cow at an agricultural show.
The caption under the picture said: Mayoress (left) does the winning honours."
There was only her and the cow in the picture.
Now that's what I call inference.

CHANGING TIMES.

DURING my Leader years I saw the newspaper go from broadsheet to tabloid and also the first coloured pictures to be used.
To me the pulse of the newspaper was the District News. Forget what disasters were happening worldwide I always believed that readers of the Rhondda Leader wanted to know "if Mrs Thomas in the next street had broken her leg after a fall? or "what was the latest news from the Women's Institute?".
Another popular section of the newspaper was the letters page and the "I Remember That" section when people

would send in school pictures among others taking Rhondda donkey's years ago.

As the old saying goes:"Nostalgia is not a thing of the past." The Leader's circulation figures at one time was always between the 12,000 and 13,000 mark but the readership figures were much higher than that.

The meaning of readership is this.

Mrs Jones would buy the Leader and when she had finished it she would give it to her sister in the next street.

When her sister had finished reading it she would send it to a cousin living in Scotland.

All that meant that one purchased Rhondda Leader had been read freely by two more people.

And of course there was a time when there would always be a page set aside for wedding pictures

St David's Day pictures was also another circulation boost along with the Bonny Babies competition.

Reporting on Golden Weddings and one hundred year olds was also part and parcel of my reporting life.

SO MANY GREAT STORIES.

I often used to think I was more of a social worker than a reporter when I would interview somebody in reception for what had all the hallmarks of a good story.

When I had finished I would say:"That's a great story just hang on and I'll sort out a picture."

To which the reply would be:"No,No you don't understand. I don't want this to go in the paper."

On one occasion a chap had come and wanted me to do a story on the state of his home to force the council to give him another property.

When I told him that I just couldn't do the story he said:"Right that's it".

"If you won't do the story I am going home to kill myself."

It took some frantic calls from me to make sure that didn't happen which thankfully it didn't.

I used to know what to expect whenever I got a call to say there was a certain someone waiting to see me.

I had only gone down a few stairs when I could hear some loud singing coming from the reception.

It was the one and only Billy Paul, brother of valley soccer legend Roy Paul.

Billy loved telling me stories about Roy. He was very proud of him.

What a character he was.

WHAT'S UP DOC?

SOME years back I felt a little under the weather so decided to pay a visit to a doctor.

After the doc gave me a going over he asked:"Do you smoke?"

"Nope".

"Do you drink alcohol?".

"No I don't".

"Are you working?"

"Yep."

"What job have you got?"

"I'm a newspaper reporter."

Stunned silence.

"You're a newspaper reporter and you don't drink or smoke?."

"'Fraid so."

He must have been watching too many TV programmes when chain smoking actors playing newspaper reporters hanging around bars trying to get a good story.
As for me?
Only a Vimto and a banana sandwich I'm afraid.

STAN AND HENRY.

MY job gave me the chance to interview people I thought I would never encounter.
I once was doing a story about valley born film star Sir Stanley Baker and I needed to get a comment from one of his close pals heavyweight boxing champion Henry Cooper.
I managed to get his number and made a call to which a woman answered who was the London born boxer's personal assistant.
"Can I help?" she asked.
"Can I speak to Henry Cooper please?", I asked.
"Who?"
"Henry Cooper"
"Who?" in a raised voiced.
"Hen.."
"Don't you mean SIR Henry Cooper?"
Oops.
Sir Henry did have a chat with me and he was great but I wasn't struck on his PA.

APRIL FOOL ANGER.

APRIL Fool's Day also brings back some memories.
If April 1 happened to coincide with the Leader being published then it was fun time for a spoof story.
This was one of mine...
I reported that I had been contacted by a millionaire from America named Doug Edwards.

Doug claimed that he was a distant relative of Welsh born buccaneer Robert Edwards, who died in 1762 and who was given 77 acres of largely unsettled Manhattan by Queen Anne.

Over the years there have been many stories of descendants of the pirate claiming they have the rightful title to billions of dollars worth of Lower Manhattan.

Unfortunately I am not one of them.

Anyway in the April 1 story I reported that Doug was throwing out an invite to all the people in the Rhondda with the surname Edwards to an all expenses paid holiday on his huge ranch in Texas.

Did I fool some of the readers all the time?

You'd better believe it.

No sooner than the paper had come out when I started getting calls from people with the surname Edwards eager to take up the offer.

And you wouldn't believe the abuse I received when I told them it was an April Fool joke.

One caller told me that "I had destroyed her life."

Couldn't get over that.

It was the last April Fool story I did.

REMEMBERING FAY.

IN 1995 I was told the worst blow a father could receive when my daughter Fay died of leukaemia aged 18.

For years I had interviewed family members in tragic circumstances but this time it was me who had to deal with the worst possible news.

I had my fair share of being on the other end of complaints during my years reporting for the Rhondda Leader but as is often said:"You can't please everyone".

But among all those complaints would come along a word of thanks which then made the job worthwhile.

But there was one big thank you which came my way in 1994 which was more than special.

Fay, my daughter from my second marriage, was not at all well and eventually she underwent hospital tests to find out what the problem was.

It was initially thought that Fay had aplastic anaemia but further tests proved that she had leukaemia.

For several weeks I regularly needed to take Fay to the University of Wales Hospital in Cardiff for blood transfusions while she awaited a bone marrow transplant.

It meant dividing my working hours with hospital visits while my daughter was having treatment.

Some weeks had gone by when I had a phone call to say that the managing director and the editor in chief of Celtic Press were coming to the Ponty office to speak to me.

"Oh!Oh! There may be trouble ahead," I thought.

I couldn't have been more wrong.

They were there to tell me that in appreciation of the work that I had put in, despite the stress I was under, they were offering me an all expenses paid trip to take Fay anywhere in the world she wanted to go when she had got better.

Fay was in hospital waiting for a bone marrow transplant when I gave her the news.

When I asked her where she would like to go her face lit up and she chose Disney Land in Florida.

Fay did eventually get a bone marrow transplant from someone on the Anthony Nolan register.

The bone marrow transplant failed and in January 1995 my angel of a daughter died at the age of 18.

During my reporting life I did many distressing stories on people who had lost loved ones and now it was something that I had to deal with.

I will always cherish the memories of Fay and I will always be hugely grateful for the brilliant gesture I received from the company I worked for.

AND FINALLY....

MY final reporting years with the Rhondda Leader were not the best.

The all powerful Internet had taken away some of the challenges I faced over my writing years.

No more did I need to book my place in the library to carry out research on a story I was writing instead I could crank up a computer put a name in a search engine and there it was before my very eyes.

The handwritten and typewritten letters which used to drop though the office letter box diminished to be replaced by e-mail.

And of course the stories I was writing were now on a web site which everyone kept telling me was the reporting way forward.

For me it wasn't.

I will always need to settle down on a couch and read a newspaper in hands and anyway you couldn't use a computer screen to wrap your fish and chips in.

Like any other newspaper reporter I had my contacts which would supply me with the latest lowdown on anything happening in the valley but even they were not needed because now I could go on Facebook.

Ahhhhh Facebook-what an eye opener that was.

If something was happening in the valley I needed to know about instead of firstly ringing the police I would check to see if it was on Facebook.

Mind you if I had written some of the things I read on Facebook I would be in front of a High Court Judge.

I made a lot of friends on my reporting journey and also a few enemies but I wouldn't have changed that journey for the world.

The job has given me the opportunity to meet many remarkable people and along the way, share a lot of laughter and a few tears.

There's an old saying that if you love your job you will never do a day's work and that has been very true in my case.

Over the years I have been able to make more friends than enemies and when I am sitting on the couch, eating my banana sandwiches I will enjoy reflecting on my many reporting memories.

I could fill a library with the stories that I have been able to cover down through the years.

Many people have asked me what I am going to do after hanging up my computer mouse.

When I put in my final full stop at the age of 64 it was a sense of sadness and relief.

Mind you retirement did take a bit of getting used to.

When I was working I used to wish I could retire to do the many odd jobs that needed doing around the house but now that I am finally retired I can't be bothered to do them.

Oh Well!